# Blow for Batten's Crossing

OTHER BOOKS BY THE AUTHOR

*A Giant Walked Among Them* (Non-fiction)
(Half-tall Tales of Paul Bunyan and his Loggers)
Illustrated by Marv Girard

*Rail Fences and Roosters* (Light Verse)
In collaboration with Marv Girard, who also
illustrated the book.

BOOKS BY THE POET
*These, My Singing Words*

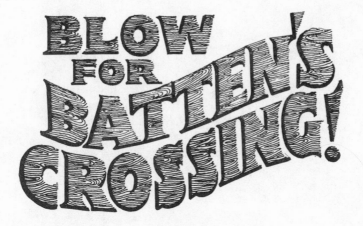

# BLOW FOR BATTEN'S CROSSING!

by

## HAZEL B. GIRARD

Photographs by the Author
Poems by Marvin Girard

A BACKWOODS ODYSSEY

GLENDON PUBLISHING
P.O. BOX 298/STERLING HEIGHTS, MI 48077

ISBN 0-934884-00-5

Library of Congress Catalog Card No. 79-54027

Cover art by George DaDeppo

Printed in the United States of America

To my dad, Jack Batten, who gave me high clouds to grow up on and hills to come home to. And to Mother who taught me to keep my feet on the ground.

# CONTENTS

*Blow for Batten's Crossing!*

# ILLUSTRATIONS

# ACKNOWLEDGMENTS

With grateful appreciation to EAST MICHIGAN TOURIST ASSOCIATION for two photographs:

THE MICHIGAN LUMBERJACK MONUMENT
AU SABLE "HIGH ROLLWAYS"

To *Bay City Times* (Bay City, Michigan), for permission to use portions of H. B. G. columns previously printed under the editorship of Kenneth Duncan.

To *Detroit Free Press* for miscellaneous paragraphs excerpted from her stories used by the late State Editor, Donald Schram.

And to *Outdoors Magazine* for privilege to reprint her article "They Live Again" which appears partially in chapter of book under "Silver Jack Was One of Them."

# INTRODUCTION

## BIG MITTEN THOUGHTS

I left my heart
  somewhere in Michigan,
I gave it
  to a lake
  and a seagull
  and a foghorn.
My heart is a summer wind
  strumming sad songs
  on a pine tree harp.

I left my heart
  somewhere in Michigan,
A river named Au Sable
  borrowed it
  and never gave it back.
I left my heart
  with a rail fence
  and a silent meadow
  and autumn
  somewhere in Michigan.

My heart is a squaw moon
  weaving sleep blankets
  for the night,
My heart is a red mackinaw
  and a six-foot lumberjack
  somewhere in Michigan.

*—Marvin Eugene Girard*

# Blow for Batten's Crossing

# 1

# SPARE THE ROD
# AND SPOIL THE REDHEAD

IT WAS SOMEWHERE BETWEEN THE AGES OF
seven-come-'leven when I made a couple trips to the woodshed when I didn't "fetch in" any wood. Mother accom-
panied me on the one expedition and Dad on the other.
Mother's accompaniment was much more impressive, also
more imprintive.

It all happened the summer the house had been re-
shingled, and the old shingles had been piled in the woodshed for winter kindling. So there wasn't any dearth of
"scutching" material around. Here a shingle. There a
shingle. Everywhere a shingle. Absolutely no shilly-shally-
ing about the shingles.

I wondered the rest of the summer just why the house
had to have a new roof anyway—the old red cedar shingles
had plenty of wear left in their fibers yet. They were as
good as the day they stood as trees in the cedar swamps.

It was the pelican verse that got me in wrong with

Mother. Remember it? Written by Dixon Lanier Merritt, it went something like this:

> "A wonderful bird is the pelican
> His bill will hold more than his belican
> He can take in his beak
> Food enough for a week
> But I'm dammed if I can see how the helican."

Mother had warned, forewarned and rewarned me if she ever caught me saying it just one more time there would be a trip to the woodshed involved. I had contaminated the kids at school without the 200-pound Scotch teacher "catchin' on" and the baby at home was adeptly picking it up. The baby was twins, so probably the offense was doubly bad.

Mother was right behind me, unawaringly, as I rendered my own version that went something like this:

> "I wonder how the helican
> The pelican
> Can put so much in his belican . . ."

Mother geezled me by the collar with one good hand, and true, and by the seat of the rompers with the other. No mistake about it, we went to the woodshed. Here a shingle. There a shingle. Everywhere a shingle. But Mother used only one, rightly placed, and with plenty of amperage. There was a bucksaw laying over a sawbuck, and Mother tossed the bucksaw aside and turned me in proper juxtaposition over the sawbuck. Wham! Bang! Bingo! The cedar swamps of the universe never grew better shingles than the one Mother used with such startling success.

It was watching the fleecy clouds go by, slowly by, that elevated Dad's ire. It was the summertime duty of little H. B. to keep the harvest hands supplied with drinking water, once or twice an hour, depending on the yeast act the mercury was putting on. A gallon jug, filled with the coldest water that could be jerked, coaxed or siphoned out of

18

the old pump was toted to the hired men with startling regularity.

I feel a deep kindred sympathy every time I see a boy at a circus toting water to an unfillable, unquenchable elephant. I could never understand it—just a swallow or two of water was all Dad ever took. He poured a bit over his wrist to cool his pulse and he was as cool as a chilblained cucumber. But the hired hands just drank and drank. And then they'd set the jug down, pick it up again and drink some more. In my deepest, most melancholy moments, I used to wish a couple of them would fall in the Au Sable River sometime. Not to be permanently drowned, of course, but the immersion prolonged enough so they'd get their fill of cold water for once.

On this particular scorching day in question, two o'clock slipped by while I lay prone under the crabtree lookin' up through the branches. Dreaming, watching, time-killing —thinking so hard and so far away, and yet thinking about nothing at all. Two o'clock went by, three o'clock went by.

I looked up and saw Dad striding his long tote-road steps across the orchard, straight toward the crabtree. And though he had never whipped me in his life, something told me this sequence was going to be different. Straight to the woodshed I headed, of all places! Here a shingle. There a shingle. Everywhere a shingle. To the right and to the left, thicker'n ticks on a hound in August.

Dad picked up a heavy-duty shingle and hit me a couple swats where he thought it would do the most good, and proceeded to give me a verbal goin'-over. "Humpin' Nellie!" he said in his usual shanty boy vernacular: "Just who do you think you are? . . . By the great horned spoons! Don'tcha know it's a blisterin' hot day and the men are sweatin' clean right out of their shirts. . . ."

He sat on the sawbuck and I sat on the chopping block, and he proceeded with a verbal spanking that hurt worse than a whole cedar swamp of shingles . . . Said it was all right to keep your head in the clouds if you managed to keep your feet on the ground. He said he hated lazy people and he didn't want a young'n' of his growin' up to be a dodderin', dreamin' no-gooder who got their livin' by spongin' off other people's hard work. "Humpin' Nellie!" . . . Didn't Mother work like a horse? And Pearl, and Amy and Beulah? . . . Well . . . didn't they? Who did I think I was anyway—Ethel Barrymore?

Dad said the gravy train had pulled out of the station and it was time to get to work—mix a little work with my spare time. . . . Go out in the garden and weed the onions, water the chickens or take 'em some sour milk mebbe . . . spell Beulah off with the churning—do something, anything. . . . Humpin' Nellie! but lay under a tree and get dreamy-lookin' as a sick cow. "Time to wake up and see the light!" he suggested with enthusiasm.

He tossed the red cedar shingle back on the pile and started for the pump. I held the jug and Dad manipulated the pump handle. We filled the jug and emptied it, filled it again and emptied it, and finally with water in it cold enough to appease the tonsils of a polar bear, we started for the hayfield. To the hayfield and the "harvest hands" with their unquenchable thirsts.

We had gone through the barnyard and through a field and not a word had been spoken. Dad looked at me and I looked at him. He winked. I slipped my freckled hand in his and he gave it a Methodist preacher squeeze. And suddenly I felt so guilty that he had to leave his work and come all the way to the house to do work I should have performed on schedule without fail. . . . And such a day, too. Hot July weather. July-nudging-August weather, and so hot even the crickets were hysterical.

But, somehow, already Dad had forgotten all about everything. He told me he had but two or three more loads of hay to get in the barn and his haying would be done for another year. "Holy ole Mackinaw!" . . . he sure hoped the storm clouds held off till night. . . . Said he hadn't killed a bird all season, and that he'd surely saved

Photo by H. Girard

Dad said it was all right to keep your head in the clouds
if you managed to keep your feet on the ground.

some by using the scythe close to the fence rows instead of using the mower.

We passed the 30-acre field, the pride of Dad's heart and the triumph of his struggles with the good earth. And it had been a good earth just sometimes, not always. Not a stump or a boulder marred its surface. It was thirty acres incorporated into one big field, and that, in a section of the country—difficult timber country, where pine stumps stood out like muscles on Paul Bunyan, was really an agricultural achievement.

Dad said he hoped to build another stretch of rail fence leading down to the pasture gully, and then he'd have 420 rods of rail fencing in that lane. Said, in his mind, he didn't think there was anything prettier than bob-whites perched on an old rail fence a'yelling their heads off. I said it seemed to me that just the rail fence alone without the birds was pretty swell to look at. Said I betcha the time would come when people would be crazy about rail fences, and those who had 'em would never tear 'em down, and those who didn't have 'em would hate their wires fences 'cause they weren't so woodsy-looking. I betcha, they would, I betcha!

Back in those days I was always saying: "I betcha!" And I didn't have a thing to bet—a few little calico, home-made dresses, some barefoot sandals, some black sateen bloomers, but still I was always saying: "I betcha!"

We arrived at the hayfield, and truly the men were "sweatin' right out of their shirts." One of them had taken his shirt off and hung it on the masthead of the hayrack. Somehow, all of a sudden, I didn't hate him so badly. He stood there on top of that load of hay with the clouds silhouetted against his strong bare shoulders. He looked rugged and substantial—like the old rail fence down the lane. He looked fearless and prodigiously happy.

. . . And I'd hated him because he was always so sweaty-looking . . . "Shame, shame on you, little brat!" something kept saying inside of me. "That man helps your dad with all the hard work of getting the hay in the barn

... And I said to Dad I thought the rail fence
without the bob-whites was pretty swell to look at.

to feed the cows next winter. Good clover hay to make them give good milk. Who ever begrudged you any milk to drink? Good Jersey milk! . . . Haven't you always had all the milk you wanted to drink . . . Well, haven't you?"

I looked at the other hired man. And, somehow, he didn't look so despicable to me either. He tipped up the jug and drank and drank. He set it down, and his Adam's apple gyrated up and down. Up again went the jug and he drank some more. But somehow, all at once, I didn't mind his "bald-headed haircut" quite so much. He always wore his hair cut right down to the bone—looked like a skull and crossbones, only without the crossbones.

It had always been surprising to me how his bereft skull seemed to generate floods of perspiration, which he snapped back from his brow with a forefinger, used in the manner of a squeegee. Somehow, now, I didn't even mind that gesture. Maybe sweatin' was a messy business, but certainly it was honorable. . . . Right that minute, I understood what Dad had meant when he suggested: "Time, kid, to wake up and see the light!"

## 2

# THE MILK RUN

FEW KIDS TODAY EVER HAVE THE PLEASURE, the high privilege, of living on a farm where the main artery of a railroad runs between the house and the barn, and the cultivated acres of the farm proper.

Back on our farm at "Batten's Crossing," the little A.S.&N.W. (The Au Sable and North Western Railroad) did just that. On one side of the narrow-gauge track—one like you see on TV on the Hooterville run, was the house, the woodshed, the chicken coop and its fenced-in yard. And, oh yes, the privy. Naturally. A trip there in the dead of winter, with snow knee-high, was like going with Santa Claus at Christmas time on his junket up around the Bering Straits. No matter how fast your track record, you were frozen for hours afterward.

On the other side of the tracks were the two barns, one called the "Old Barn" because of its vintage. Part of it had been made from logs, all uniform in size, about 12-14 inches in diameter. The building had never been painted, but was a weathered, time-beaten color designated in modern color paint charts of today as "Nantucket gray." And there was the "New Barn"—a much bigger structure that housed Dad's prancing horses, with their high rumps and high spirits. There were huge areas for the hay mows. Part of a hay mow extended over the horse stable, making a wonderful insulated housing, a first-floor apartment for the equine members of the family. There was a nice smell permeating that barn—a pungent, horsey, leathery smell, mixed with the spicy fragrance of red and white clover hay in the mows.

The granary, housing the threshed grain, was also on the same side of the railroad tracks, with its huge bins of wheat, oats, barley, speltz, buckwheat and shelled corn. This was the "hang-out" for a couple of family cats that kept the rat and mouse population of the premises to a minus zero.

The cow stable was in the old barn—but with no milking parlors, I-gollys! The cows—Ole Cherry, Pinky, Rosy, Trixie, Anabelle, Abigail and the rest were tied to a manger, lined up like inches on a ruler. Outside was the inevitable "manure pile." First travelable day in springtime, this bovine refuse was spread over the ground to fertilize the good earth. And sometimes, some years, not-so-good earth.

We kids never did figure out how all the Canadian thistles managed to "crop up" through the beautiful fields of red and white clover. Came up by the dozens, by the hundreds. Dad always kept the fence rows meticulously cleaned by cutting all weeds with the scythe. We wondered if the birds carried and scattered some of the seeds. We wondered maybe if some of the stupid cows—they weren't all as smart as Ole Cherry, could have eaten them, and the seeds passed through their four stomachs, and had seeded the ground via the fertilizer route. We never knew, and

26

The hired man picked up the jug
and drank and drank—and drank.

could only guess. Dad didn't know either and, it seemed to us, he always had the correct answer to most everything.

The little A.S.&N.W. train went by the Home Place about 8:30 in the morning and returned at 4:30 in the afternoon. It had the engineer aboard, the firemen, the brakeman, the conductor and the cook in the caboose. It carried one passenger car, the caboose and plenty of flat cars. When it returned in the afternoon, all flat cars were loaded with freshly-cut sawlogs that had been picked up at Russell, McKinley and points at the end of the line, to be taken to the sawmills at Au Sable and Oscoda. It was legend that the conductor and brakeman always went rabbit hunting while the flat cars were being loaded in McKinley.

The "Old Barn" had a tool shed housing all the necessary tools and small implements used around the farm. All kinds of saws from keyhole to seven-foot crosscut saws were here. Hammers, screw drivers, planes of all sizes were lined up neatly on shelves, like sterilized instruments in a dental cabinet. There were post-hole diggers, fence stretchers, hand corn planters, scythes, cradles, sickles and an assortment of hoes.

Some of us kids who were good at making doll clothes thought we were pretty something with a hammer and saw. And we had bird houses to show for our carpentry prowess. All tools were supposed to be off-limits to us, and Dad always knew when someone had "been messing around" with any of them. Said he could always tell by the "feel" of them. They were supposedly "off limits" as much as using his straight razor for cutting cardboard.

One sure way Mother had of getting chores done about the place, like getting a fence repaired around the chicken yard, or a new fence post put in by the front gate maybe, was to say she was going to do it herself. The use of tools was on the "off limits" list for her, too. So, the job got done before she could dull a saw or wrestle the handle off a hammer.

In the dead of wintry blizzards when huge snowdrifts piled along the tracks, the railroad snowplow went ahead of the train and cleared the tracks.

One time the snowplow itself couldn't make it through the dense snowdrifts. The crew shoveled and shoveled, but like Uncle DeLormey's sweenied horse, the snowplow just ran out of poo, and had no pep, no pickup. It couldn't go ahead, and it couldn't go backward. It was between two banks of land along the tracks that had drifted full. It was about a city block away from our place, and we could hear the puffing, anguished suffering of the little narrow-gauge engine.

The conductor and the brakeman knocked on the kitchen door and asked Mother if she could spare some supplies for them. Their edibles were gone; the men were exhausted and starved. They said they had the dishes and cooking utensils in the caboose, just needing something to cook. She didn't have to be choosey, they said.

Mother told them "Most certainly!" and told them to come back in 15-20 minutes. In that time she loaded a couple big baskets (bought from the Indians in their settlement the summer before). There were three loaves of homemade bread, a two-quart blue-green fruit jar of pickled crabapples, some lean side-pork freshly fried, 3 dozen hard-boiled eggs. There was a pound of homemade butter, a couple jars of her precious wild raspberry jam. There were a couple big fruit jars of Jersey milk, a couple dozen fat sugar cookies baked for school lunches, and a couple gallons of piping hot coffee with sugar and real cream. The conductor asked how much he owed her, and Mother said: "Just make it a couple dollars."

A few days later the train stopped at the crossing, and the conductor knocked again at the kitchen door. He was returning the baskets, the fruit jars, and the linen towels Mother had smothered around the "vittles." He stood there in his blue uniform, with gold braid on it, and had a covered tin bucket, two-quart size, in his hand—and wondered if it would be possible to get two quarts of "that good Jersey milk" every day. He had it all figured out—he'd stand on the bottom step of the passenger coach, and one of the children could pass the can of milk to him. He'd have the train come to a dead stop so there'd be no danger of one of the children getting accidentally hurt. He wanted a two-pound "print" of butter every Saturday and a quart of cream. Little H. B. was selected as the milk passer because she was tall and lanky, and had long windmill arms that hung to her knees. There'd be no trick to the passing milk routine. The conductor, Billy Ellis, had the money ready every Saturday in an envelope. He pulled it out of his blue uniform pocket just before he reached for the dairy supplies.

Once the conductor asked us kids to pick him some dandelion greens. It was early springtime, and Mother showed us the right kind to gather, the tender leaves from the very young plants. After we had picked a good bushel of them, Mother looked them over carefully and discarded any she thought might be the slightest bit tough. She packed them tenderly in one of the huge baskets in which she had previously packed their edibles when they were snowbound. There was no aluminum foil at that time, of course, but Mother made the greens a sleeping bag out of waxed paper and sprinkled them with cold, cold water from the pump, and kept them in the root cellar till train time.

Billy Ellis, the conductor, gave us a brand new two-dollar bill. The guys who discovered gold at Sutter's Creek couldn't have been more jubilant than we were, the sole owners of a two-dollar bill. And ours! It had a picture of Thomas Jefferson on it, and he seemed to be looking right at us, eyeball to eyeball.

And there was the time "Mr. Ellis" (Mother always insisted we call him "Mr. Ellis" even in conversation around home) asked us to pick some dandelion blossoms. Mother said she bet a nickel he "was up to something." Probably going to make himself a batch of dandelion wine. We kids picked dandelion blossoms by the hundreds, by the thousands, it seemed, and garnered another brand new picture of Thomas Jefferson. We even chewed some new yellow dandelions to figure out how Mr. Ellis' wine might taste.

And there was another time when he ordered some "Morel mushrooms." Since we kids didn't know a morel mushroom from a toadstool, Mother took us to the woods and showed us what they looked like, growing real crazy thick under the poplars. These, too, were "picked over" to make sure they were the best that could be found. Those that had a little vintage on them, and might be a little tough, she saved for the family. She tenderly fried them in butter—they were the first mushrooms we kids had ever eaten, and we thought they were wonderful . . . we hoped Mr. Ellis sure was enjoying the very choice ones we had picked for him. Mother probably had had another reason for scrutinizing his mushrooms so carefully. She wanted positively to make sure, in our anxiety to find so many mushrooms, we hadn't maybe slipped in some toadstools. To have poisoned "Mr. Ellis" would have been one of the worst things that could possibly have happened to us.

Some folks leave their hearts in San Francisco; some have left their footprints in a cement sidewalk. We kids left our hearts in a two-quart milk container, and a big Indian basket.

Years later, when some of us kids had completed all the schooling that was provided in the country school, we "went away to school"—Beulah stayed with brother George in Jackson for four years; H. B. and the twins stayed with sister Pearl in Ann Arbor. When we went home for Christmas vacation, the brakeman stopped the A.S.&N.W. train right smack-dab at Batten's Crossing. Right at the Home Place. Back where it had all started. Back to the frozen coot and hern of the wooded creek flats; back to Dad's beloved 30-acre field laying dormant under its blanket of northern Michigan's blue-white clean snow; back to Mother's root house loaded with garden stowaways; and to the upstairs bedroom with its frosted frescoes on the window

31

panes and the patchwork quilts on the bed, and the scratching of the branches of the giant crabapple tree against the side of the house. Back to "Batten's Crossing" for Christmas—to the waiting, anxious arms of Dad and Mother, and to the home of Mr. and Mrs. John W. Batten.

## 3

# HOT IRON AND TOBACCO JUICE

DAD WAS SIX FEET, PLUS TWO OR THREE INCHES
tall. He had the longest lap, it seemed, I ever saw. It easily
held four of the youngest kids: Beulah, H. B. and the twins.

Beulah had red hair, and green eyes exactly like Dad's.
They had a liquid look like a pool in the sunlight catching
up the green color of a willow tree on the bank. She had a
lovely pink complexion that never seemed to tan or
freckle, even in the scorchiest heat of dog days. It just
kept a wild rose, outdoorsy, wind-blown look all summer
long. She was a pretty girl, but not the spectacular pretti-
ness the twins had with their straight black hair and their
black, black eyes. They were eyes that always seemed to
be laughing, even though their faces were sober. It was
disgusting for a pair of kids to be that pretty. And two of
them at once, exactly alike. Made you think you were
seeing double. And you were.

The less said about H. B., the better. She, too, was red-headed—a bright, vibrant red, the exact color of freshly-washed carrots. It was the color known in the circus world as "clown red." And there was an impish pug nose that headed straight upstairs, always looked like it was smelling something in the attic. But worst of all were the freckles. By the dozens and by the hundreds. Hundreds and hundreds. On the hands and arms, the forehead, the back of the neck, the whole physiognomy. Once Beulah and I tried to count them, putting down a mark every time we reached a hundred. We had gotten the count well over 2,000, and hadn't gotten off the hands and arms. We gave up. It was just too much. There were too, too many.

It was downright pitiful for a kid to be that homely. Certainly the homeliest kid in the family, and far and away the homeliest kid in the whole school. All the mirrors reflected the same sad story—the old one on the back veranda, outside the kitchen door where the hired men "washed up" before mealtime, the bedroom and parlor mirrors—all retold the same message. (Once I accidentally came upon one of the hired men who was immersing some newborn kittens in a galvanized pail of water—and real quick-like I had the morbid, melancholy feeling, a fleeting half-second thought, that maybe that should have happened to me the day I was born.)

Those freckles arrived in March, and disappeared only through the coldest winter months. Just seemed to go under cover to wait for sunshine and the bluebirds. But the first warm days in March when the winds blew a tepid brisk-ness, they started to arrive. First of all were a couple that appeared on the right hand between the knuckles of the index and forefinger. They were half as big as copper pennies—side by side they appeared, always the first of the season, and had been doing it for years. I lovingly called them Aggie and Maggie.

The kids at school knew about the two freckles that appeared every March as unerringly as the swallows came back to Capistrano on the 21st of March without fail, and they'd be looking for them. One morning I woke up, and there they were. Same place, same size, same brownness, side by side like Dad's horses, Champ and Jess, harnessed up for the day.

I kept the right hand in my pocket or sat at my desk with the left hand covering the right one. Came second recess, mid-afternoon, and one of the girls asked about Aggie and Maggie. I merely nodded affirmatively they had arrived, but I acted reluctant to give them a viewing. The girl offered me a penny for a look-see, and all at once I was in business.

Next day, same thing—Aggie and Maggie were kept in seclusion. They just played plumb hard-to-get. I had the dress pocket treasury up to eleven cents when one of my sisters, I never knew which one, reported it to Mother. The next day, real pronto, as soon as I got to school, she made me give back my ill-gotten gains.

Sitting on Dad's Abraham Lincoln-like lap, we heard many things. Always, by request, was the singing of shanty boy songs. "Fair Charlotte by the Mountain Side," and "Ole Leather Breeches" and that favorite of all ex-shanty boys: "The Jam on Garry's Rock."

He'd tell us about the cooks in the chuckhouse at the lumber camps. Paddy McGraw and "Beany" Stevens who flipped flapjacks in every chow emporium along the Au Sable. They could flip a pancake with one hand and flop a twenty-inch steak with the other. "Beany" Stevens was called "Beany" because he knew so much about beans. Beans were always available when Beany was around. There were beans baked with salt pork, beans baked with venison spare ribs, beans baked with molasses, beans baked with brown sugar, beans baked with white sugar, beans baked with applesauce, beans baked with wild honey, beans baked with other beans. We kids laughed and laughed. We thought Dad's stories were wonderful.

Mother would sit in her rocking chair and sew on buttons, or knit. It was a small rocking chair without arms,

35

just right for mending, knitting, patching or sewing carpet rags. She'd sit back and never say a word, just mind her business at hand. Probably she was glad to have someone entertain the yakity kids for a while. The knitting was never finished. She knit black woolen stockings for the girls going to school, made with shiny black yarn and knit long enough to come up well over the knees. And there were mittens and more mittens. There was no orlon or acrylic yarns then, always it was four-ply worsted she used. She made mittens of double yarn for extra warmth: red and green, red and black, red and gray—always red made an appearance. There were no shades with festive names like Caribbean blue, Fiesta orange, Midnight burgundy, Arbutus pink, and such.

She knit heavy mittens for Dad, usually of gray yarn, and they were also made double-knit for warmth. She knit "wristlets" for him because he was so long-armed he never could find shirts long enough in the sleeves, so the wristlets made with knit two, purl two pattern gave a stretchy comfortable covering for the vulnerable cold area between the shirt cuffs and the mittens. And there were the long scarves she knitted for the kids going to school. They wound around the neck two or three times, and were usually made with stripes in them and with fringes on the ends. With a stocking cap on pulled down well over the eyebrows, and a long scarf on with a circle of it pulled up over your face leaving just the eyes visible, you paddled to school and got the best teaching a kid ever had.

It was hard going through a deep snow that had fallen during the night and completely filled the road. We kids used to walk along the fences at the side of the road, and walk backward. The fence served as a guide in the right direction, and by walking backward it kept the icy wind blasts out of our faces.

Quite often Dad would hitch up Champ and Jess and take us to school in the sleigh which was equipped with a wagon box which had a foot of straw in the bottom for warmth. Occasionally when the snow was too deep, the horses couldn't make their way through it. They would get down, sprawled out like turtles. This always annoyed Dad to ardent disgust, and he'd say: "You kids are all as stubborn as your mother." We always had a perfect attendance record at school year after year for being neither tardy nor absent, and weren't about to break it. Always we had to be there, and our stubbornness won us a present at the end of the school year. The reward was usually a book about an industrious kid or an animal that didn't have a mean bone in its body.

Once at school, the first task was to make a trip to the out-house in back of the school. There was a matched pair in opposite corners of the yard; one designated "Boys" and the other "Girls." They were strictly utilitarian, not near as nice as the one we had at home. Shucks, no! The one at home had a seating space that had been planed and sanded satin-smooth. It even had three different size indentions—like the Papa-bear size, a Mama-bear size, and Baby-bear size. The walls were white-washed, and had a mirror hanging on the wall. One of us once hung a hanging pot from the ceiling, filled with wild ferns. Dad hit his head an awful crack on it once, and that was the end of our decorating of privies.

Once when we were walking to school—along the fence and walking backward, taking one step at a time and the wind blowing us back two steps, I mentioned to Beulah that it was "one hell of a way to get smart." Beulah already had acquired brains she couldn't use, a miscellaneous polyglot of information covering diversified fields of knowledge. She learned quickly, and retained it forever. She even bowled the crusty teacher over with her retention of poetry. Take her interpretation of Celia Thaxter's poem:

> "Across the lonely beach we flit
> One little sandpiper and I
> And fast we gather bit by bit
> The scattered driftwood, bleached and dry."

Beulah told H. B. she couldn't understand how anyone who loved beautiful things like sunsets, waving grain in the fields and cows wading in the creek, could have "such a dirty little mouth."

She made it so convincing you felt you were right there with Celia. She knew so many lovely poems, and was plumb full of lovely thoughts. She lowered a verbal boom on me, said she couldn't figure out how I, who loved beautiful trees, sunsets, waving grain, cows wading in the creek, rail fences and bob-whites, could have "such a dirty little mouth."

She promptly reported the incident to Mother at night, and Mother, real quick-like, dropped to the conclusion I'd picked up the vernacular at the blacksmith's shop. The smithy's place was a quarter mile from home, and we kids used to stop in occasionally and watch the horses being shod. Good ole Edd Boddy, the smithy, didn't seem to mind. He'd let us pump the bellows and take time to explain to us he wasn't hurting a horse when he trimmed its hooves before putting the shoes on. He explained it would feel good to the horse to have the growth removed, and said sometimes horses became crippled because their feet weren't properly trimmed. He chewed tobacco, and sometimes when he was hammering something on the anvil would spit toward the flaming fire. He just never missed, whether he spat head-on or sidewise. Once when I was pumping the bellows and had acquired a good mastery of the spitting routine, I got reported on that one, too.

Anyway, after the swear word on the way to school, the smithy's shop was "off limits" to all of us, both to and from school. A kid misses a place like that. We missed the horsey smell of the smithy's shop, with the acrid smell of corncob pipes smoking, and the burnt leather smell of Edd's big leather apron that hung all the way to the floor. It was years and years old, and still serving its purpose.

When I reassured Mother the swear word hadn't come from the blacksmith shop at all, and that I wouldn't use it again, the visitation rights were reinstated. "Just keep out of his way," she admonished. "Edd's a busy man, and can't be pestered with kids hangin' around and asking dozens of nosy questions."

The next morning when we started to school, and had just gotten outside the front gate, we could hear the stacatto hammering on the anvil from up the road. We ran all the way to Edd's, stopped in just momentarily—and left him a huge Northern Spy apple.

# 4

# MY HORSE-TRADING UNCLE

UNCLE DELORMEY AND AUNT MARTY LIVED on a 40-acre farm just beyond the blacksmith shop. He kept three or four milking cows, and did farming the easy way—just didn't worry about anything.

I do not recall that Uncle DeLormey ever had a well at his place, that is a well with a pump. He had something much more unusual and picturesque. No one else had a possession like it in all the neighborhoods around. It was his conquest, and his alone. If it wasn't the most convenient and most expedient contraption in the world, he owned something everyone else wished they had. He actually had "an old oaken bucket that hung in the well" right outside the kitchen door.

Possibly, at one time he had toyed with the idea of digging a well, and when he had "gotten down" 14-15 feet he had found an underground spring, a perpetual spring that kept dispersing icy water through the hottest

days in summer and the coldest days in winter. It just gave
and gave, and never ran dry.

"Unc" walled up the four sides of the well with sturdy
timbers, rigged up a pole system on the ground level and
fastened a heavy-duty rope to it, and fastened an oaken
bucket to the other end. The bucket was lowered into the
well and filled itself with the coldest water that could be
desired. He didn't bother figuring out a windlass system,
so one could just turn a crank and the bucket would be
raised to the top of the well, brimming over with water.
With his system, you just used the rope, manual-like,
lowered it into the well and brought it topside by the
hand-over-hand system on the rope.

It wasn't any time before the bucket accumulated a
healthy covering of moss on the outside, as did the sides of
the timbered wall. It was truly a paragraph of great fun,
lowering and hoisting that old oaken bucket filled with its
cold, cold water. Hard work, but it was fun. Unc, the
sweet-hearted codger that he really was, was real good
about always having a couple buckets of water ahead for
Marty in the kitchen so she wouldn't have to be "luggin' it
in." We kids used to often stop by on our way home from
school to see if Aunt Marty didn't need some water brought
in. A kid will do anything so they don't have to go straight
home, and it always gave us a plausible excuse.

One thing that deeply irked Uncle 'Lorm was winter.
Yearly, he got disgusted with winter waiting to do the bum's
rush, and for greening springtime to come. He liked cer-
tainties, sequences, swift changes and sure returns.

Being quite rotund, he was continually falling on the
ice. A perpetual, perennial daydreamer, he was always
sitting down in the wrong places. Aunt Marty said he always laughed in all the wrong places, too, and at the wrong
time. He held the euchre and checker championships for
miles around, and might have gotten a truly wonderful kick
out of life if he hadn't hated winter so much. Yearly, it
spoiled a good half of the year for him. He plumb hated

winter in all its interpolations, variations and ramifications. He disliked cold tea and despised ice cream. Unc used to grab a bamboo fishpole that hung under the porch eaves and disgustedly knock the icicles off the porch every morning before he put his bridgework in. It was an easy way to show his disdain for ice, and winter in general.

But part of Unc's aversion for winter was due to the fact that he was a great fisherman. And winter required too much wood-chopping. Much too much. He loved to sit and fish and dream; then again, sometimes, just sit and fish. And hating winter like he did, no one—no time, no place, ever saw Uncle DeLormey doing any ice-fishing. He might have had a really gallupsious, roarin' good time just building himself a fish shanty, and sitting and dreaming. A kerosene lantern inside the shanty would have provided ample warmth. But, shucks! there was all that work of building a shanty—taking it to location on some lake, and "spudding" a hole in the ice every time you wanted to fish, and removing the shanty from the lake at first breakup in the springtime. Somehow, it just didn't seem worth all the wear and tear. Couldn't be.

He was always waiting for summer. It was good horse-trading weather, the best of the year. Unc professed to be a keen judge of horse flesh. He bought and swapped and sold and bought again with startling regularity. Life for him was just one equine cycle after another, just one long horse race.

Once he got hooked with a rare archaic specimen that couldn't pull the hat off your head, couldn't even pull the hat band. But he turned right around and swapped that docile nag for a skittish quadruped called Dynamite. All Uncle DeLormey had to do was to show Dynamite a beer bottle, and he'd begin to whinny, arch his neck, fluff out his tail and proceed to get ready to go to town.

But Unc wasn't satisfied, no siree! He swapped Dynamite for Flossie. She was easily 99.44 per cent pure bolognie, that horse. She was what is classified in the best horse doctor books as a sweenied horse. Now a sweenied horse, to all you readers who didn't come from a long lineage of horse traders, is one that has worn out its shoulder muscles from constant contact with the collar, and has empty sagging skin wrinkles where the muscles ought to be. The sweenied horse will throw its complete struggling weight into a pull, but it's no dice! There's no pep, no pickup.

Unc wouldn't admit he'd been stung. Coaxing, strategy and time, he was sure, would make a Hercules out of Flossie. So, he put her into harness one day and stood off a ways with a piece of licorice. Floss was a devil for licorice, and Uncle DeLormey was getting dubious about his reputation for picking horses.

She threw every gram of strength against the collar. There were two reverberating pops and Flossie eclipsed from this laboring vale of tears. Unc was left standing pop-eyed, holding the licorice, and praying again: "My kingdom for a horse!"

But then there was the little matter of telling Aunt Marty. And it really was no "small matter" at all. Aunt Marty didn't, and never in her lifetime, weigh over 99 pounds. Unc called it "witch's weight." But when she stood with her hands on her lean, slender hips—and her feet wide apart, like Napoleon at the bridge, she looked as formidable as a bear trap.

Unc decided it best to break the news to her at supper. It was Wednesday—and Marty always had hot buttermilk biscuits for supper on Wednesdays, served with cold applesauce or some homemade jam. He hoped it would be raspberry jam, wild raspberry jam, no less.

Now, there was a concoction you could rhapsodize over with gusto. Uncle DeLormey had perfected that art to a fine finesse. He'd compose the compliments most copiously, pass out the platitudes, accentuate the accolades—especially about Aunt Marty's wild raspberry jam. Shucks! there wasn't anyone in Alcona County who could make "them kind of biscuits" and he doubted if anyone in the

44

whole state of Michigan could match her jam-making prowess.

We kids—and there was a big passel of us, came along like mushrooms in the springtime, were real grabbers when it came to picking berries: wild strawberries, huckleberries, and wild rambunctious blackberries whose bushes towered over our young heads. And most delicious of all were the wild raspberries.

Mother always had an abundance of jam in the root cellar for lunch pails going to school. Take homemade bread meringued with a vigorous helping of homemade butter, topped with a generous helping of wild raspberry jam—and no modern day school cafeteria lunch could touch it.

But good as we kids were at picking berries, Aunt Marty had us all beaten. She could pick with both hands at once, one moving equally as fast as the other. She could even pick cross-handed, and never miss a pluck. Better than that, she could pick berries cross-handed and keep right on talking. Pearl always made us quit "yaking" when we were picking berries. We liked a little conversation with the job, but knowing big sister Pearl, we "included it out," as Samuel Goldwyn used to put it.

In the high bushes of wild raspberries and blackberries, it was not unusual to see a wild bear feasting on the goodies. They'd stand on their hind feet, hold a branch with the biggest berries in the woods between their two front paws, and subtract every berry on the branch. They always seemed to have a penchant for finding the bushes loaded with the biggest berries in ten acres.

We kids ran away if we encountered a bear picking berries in our patch. Not Aunt Marty! She stood her ground —never turned her back on them but never slowed down her reaching routine. She never believed in backin' away from any bear that was easy to see. Many years of living with Uncle 'Lorm, it seemed, had inoculated her with bravery beyond the call of duty. She used to go home and tell him she had picked right off the same bush where the bear was eating, and she had latched onto the big ones before he did.

So, every summer Aunt Marty "put up" plenty of jam of all kinds, especially the wild raspberry jam. She didn't have a root cellar for storage, so it went on the pantry shelves. She even labeled each jar where the berries were picked—like "Camp Four Woods" or "Ferguson Woods." They were put in neat rows, and Aunt Marty kept a curtain pulled over the goodies to keep the light out of their faces.

. . . Came suppertime. Hot buttermilk biscuits, replete with wild raspberry jam, were waiting for Uncle DeLormey. Unc ate and gorged, and gorged and ate. His outpouring of "savvy" was at its best.

He pushed his chair back from the table, snapped his galluses a couple times, cleared his throat, and huskily told Aunt Marty that Flossie was no more. Poor dear Flossie! She had gone to that big equine Round-up in the skies. He would miss her terribly. Always.

Aunt Marty didn't rant and rave. She was sitting down at the time, drowned in the flood of Unc's compliments—so she couldn't draw herself up to her full whippet height, and stand with her feet wide apart like Napoleon at the bridge. She just gave him a "I could have told you so!" look that came right out with accusatory gusto, and said: "You ole fool . . . you'll never learn!"


## MAKE ME A BOY AGAIN

Make me a boy for just a day
   That's all I ask of You.
Bring back the courage of my youth
   So I can build anew
The pleasant dreams a heart will hold

Photo by H. Girard

## THE BEACHCOMBER
(Thunder Bay, Michigan)

## Blow for Batten's Crossing!

When life is sweet and good;
Make me a boy for just a day
        . . . . Oh God, but if You could!

Let me tread again, with barefoot steps,
    Those lanes of my childhood past;
Let me know again mute woodland aisles
    Where nature's spell is cast.
I long for the boyhood yesterdays
    That I thrilled to long ago
When youth was cheap and I squandered it
    On hook and line and bow.

Make me a boy for just a day,
    Is that too much to ask?
Could not You free a captive heart
    From bonds that hold it fast?
Could not You change the brittle bone
    For a frame raw, lean and strong?
Make me a boy for just a day
        . . . . Oh God, is that too long?

The bright-eyed world I lived in then
    Ended all too soon;
A laughing mouth no longer shapes
    The happy, homespun tune.
The driftwood ships I captained once
    Have found some other shore;
Harsh tides have torn my castles down
    And I will make no more.

The memories of my precious youth
    Live on and always will;
The swimming hole, the old log raft,
    The birch upon the hill.
And though I've grown old and grim and gray,
    My soul cannot refrain
From wishing its wish, that eternal wish,
    Make me a boy again!

*—Marvin Eugene Girard*

# 5

# LONESOME WHISTLE CALLING

THE TWINS WERE THE YOUNGEST IN THE FAMily. My brother, George, was the oldest. He left home shortly after the twins were born. They made seven girls in the family. Probably the very thought of seven sisters was just more than the poor guy could stand.

If the reason for his leaving home was having too many girls around, the ironic thing about it was when he got married, he had four daughters. More girls, girls, girls!

Besides, he hated the farm with an intensity he couldn't tell about—everything connected with the farm. The circuitous merry-go-round of work that was never done. Always some work left over, and more comin' up. He disliked the planting, the hoeing, the endless spraying the potato bugs, milking the cows, currying the horses, distributing the manure piles. He hated the scorching sun, and the crazy summer rains that came on without warning. Made the weeds grow faster with more hoeing comin' up, and more potato bugs a-hatching.

Positively, without one single merit, everything about the farm he disliked: the sunsets, the early morning getting-up deals, the long after-supper quietude, the unending winding-up sessions of the crickets, the croaking frogs in a nearby pond, the neighborhood dogs across the lonely acres that answered each other's barking all through the long nights. No, thank you!

He had a yen to be on the move. He had a yen for railroading. Maybe the fact that he had seen the little A. S. & N. W. trains go by the house all the days of his life preceding had something to do with it. He loved its steam, its whistle, its smell—and just the looks of a train following a pair of rails down the track.

He left home, not knowing exactly where he was going. His first letter home was from Duluth, Minnesota. He had "hired on" with a railroad, and it was going to be his life. He loved it.

He knew immediately railroading was going to be his life's work—he loved it like a sailor loves the spray of the sea. He sent money home every couple weeks, thinking the folks back there would surely be needing some. Mother never spent a dime received; every dime, every nickel of it was deposited in a savings account for him. When he married, he had an unexpected windfall. He progressed up the ladder, and was general yardmaster of the Michigan Central lines in Jackson, Michigan, at time of his retirement. We kids thought it was really something that he and his family could travel on a "pass" and not have to pay a cent. That was really living, really "living it up" in our instant arithmetic.

Ida, the oldest girl in the family, married when she was quite young. Married a "section hand." They were the men who worked on the railroad and traveled the rails every day by pumping a "hand car" and always checking and replacing ties along the tracks—looking, always carefully scrutinizing, for loose spikes that may appear along the tracks where they're fastened to the railroad ties.

It seems she met her husband at the well—our well, with its cold, cold water. The section hands stopped there a couple times a day to replenish the water in their jugs. Sometimes they ate their lunches in the nearby orchard.

At the pump, she met him, I-gollys! surrounded with its fragrant sweet clover, higher than the pump, higher than her young shoulders. Maybe it was the fragrance of the blossoming sweet clover; maybe it was the pure-tasting cold water, but she fell heels over head in love with the man "working on the railroad." We kids didn't know it at the time but we were getting a "gandy dancer" for a brother-in-law.

Dad and Mother weren't too happy about the match, thought he was a little too old for her. But they reasoned, practical-like, she surely could do much, much worse. He was a steady worker; they knew he never missed a day's work regardless of the weather. And he didn't drink, smoke or swear—so was bound to be a "good provider." Maybe he did have a name that was hard to pronounce, and was the only one in all the neighborhoods around who had a name ending in "ski," but they liked the way he always said "Mr. Batten" and "Mrs. Batten." It certainly showed he owned a wealth of good manners.

Dad had 100 acres of land to farm, with the aid of six farmer's daughters. All lithe and lean, and not a pound of fat on any of them, all skinny as rolled umbrellas. It was enough to make a farmer drink an overdose of "Paris Green," the spray used on the potato bugs.

But Dad loved the farm. He had known it when it was all virgin forests—and by sweat, tired muscles and tenacity, and the help of a pair of gallant horses, and a courageous woman in the house who worked as hard as the horses, had cleared the forest acres and made them ready for the plow. Mother often told us kids that the first few years when she knew the place, she had often detoured around wild bears on her way to the privy. Said she wasn't scared. They didn't seem to look at her, and she didn't look at them. Each one

51

Dad's livestock was sleek and of happy disposition.

went about their own business. Mother said she thought the bears probably knew she was pregnant and felt sorry for her.

Dad had the reputation of being an excellent farmer. His fences were always kept in good repair; his fields were fertile and repaid him with good harvests. His livestock was sleek and of happy disposition, never a rib showing on any of his animals. His horses were his pride and joy, high-rumped and cadaverous, filled with oats and guile, and probably "ran away" more than any horses in Alcona County. One couldn't say they were nervous and skittish, they were just busting out all over with the joy of living.

Dad had those horses spoiled rotten. They did a good day's work for him, and he was always telling them about it. They were always nuzzling around his pockets for candy, and would always find some. Pink wintergreen lozenges usually. They wouldn't eat them, just suck on them and make 'em last a long time. He'd pet their noses and say: "Nice Champ! . . . Nice Jess!"

Dad usually kept 8-10 cows. Good milking cows that gave and gave, thought about the lush clover growing in the creek flats, and then gave some more. Mother called it "stripping the cows" well, siphoning the last drop of milk they had to give. All the girls could milk, but a couple of them usually did the supper dishes while the others milked cows. Dad curried the horses, and Mother often worked in her garden after supper. It was a cool time of the day and pleasant in the garden. Birds were singing in the orchard in a vesper chorus; crickets were winding up their rattles for the night. One thing that always annoyed Mother was when one of the girls while milking would have a cow kick, and spill a whole 10-quart bucket of milk. The cats would come a-runnin', and so would Mother. She always knew when she saw cats take off for the barnyard, in unison, there had been an accident. She didn't think too much of the long fingernails some of us girls were trying to grow, and we always got blamed for pinching the cows. "Just look

Dad's horses did a good day's work for him
and he was always telling them about it.

at all that beautiful milk!" she'd say in bewilderment, almost in tears.

Four seasons around the Batten place didn't mean the name of a posh restaurant, although the quality of the cuisine furnished there would have paralleled that of the eating emporiums of the whole big, food-conscious world. And four seasons didn't mean the name of four seasonal segments of the year, although the extravagant beauty of the seasons was unforgettable as each season slipped into the next one. Four seasons merely meant the work pattern that continually went on as weeks tagged long working days, and months tail-gated the weeks. Somehow, it all blended together to make a montage of work that was never, never done.

Certainly Dad always had chores and "things to do" even on rainy days. Scythes to sharpen, saws to sharpen, hoes to sharpen, harness to be mended, handles to be re-placed in hammers and axes. Everyone knows that a wo-man's work is never done, and certainly Johannah Batten never got caught up with hers. Dad said she "fussed too much" every time she churned, in making the famous "prints" of butter that were her trademark. She'd take the side of the butter ladle and create a spear of wheat on top of the print. Or make a morning glory blossom, a maple leaf or a squash blossom. She didn't "go for" the objects of art some of the kids were always coaxing her to make— like caterpillars, Ole Cherry's head with her cowbell, the privy with ivy vines growin' over it, and the like. Dad used to tell Mother she was sure "one awful putterer." He'd say: "Throw the food on the table—it'll taste just as good . . . all be gone in five minutes anyway!" Probably he was think-ing of the plank-board tables in the chuckhouse at the lum-ber camps he had known in these other days. Mother, in growing season, always had a vase of flowers on the long oblong dining-room table, and always a huge vase of flowers on the mammoth red sideboard, atop a fancy crocheted doily. Fastidious, perfectionist Mother, she didn't believe in slapstick housekeeping.

Rachael Carson, she of *Silent Spring,* would have loved our mother, and the way she shied away from using poisonous chemicals in her garden. DDT had not yet been born but Mother didn't miss it anyway. She saved the soap suds from the long washday sessions, and put it on her garden plants after supper. It was soap suds that had initiative and authority behind it, potent suds from the yellow "Oak Leaf" soap. She was never bothered with thrips, borers, cutworms, aphids, leaf hoppers, and such. She conquered all, test tubes be hanged!

The haying at that time was done by mowing. Hay-baling had not yet come into being. After the mowing came the raking of the hay. All the girls excelled at that task, raking the new-mown hay into windrows. The hired man "cocked" the hay and made it into "hay doodles." The important thing to do was to get the hay doodles into the barn before they got rained on. If a downpouring rain drenched them for a couple of days, they had to be torn apart and let the sun dry them thoroughly because it was dangerous to put damp hay in the barn. "Spontaneous combustion," it was called when a fire resulted.

Seemed there was one thing the hired men couldn't do to please Dad, and that was to properly "build" a load of hay. Hay pitched up to the man on the hayrack had to be placed right, correctly right, to give the load a proper balance. The hay had to be properly distributed on the hay-rack so the load wouldn't be lopsided, and the whole thing slide off on the way to the barn.

Dad was a true architect at building a load of hay. No load of his ever went slipping and sliding to the ground. It was a waste of time and doubled the work when a load of hay capsized and had to be reloaded. Then, too, it plumb scared the wintergreen calm right out of the horses.

Once when one of the hired men had been the Frank Lloyd Wright of a load of hay—and it had toppled over before it got halfway to the barn, Dad just calmly walked away from the mishap, and left the two hired men to wrestle with it the best they could, without his help.

He strode his long tote-road strides toward the house, and into the kitchen. He was hoppin' disgusted, and had departed from the scene rather than speak his piece. "That pair of clowns have to be as dumb as a couple gillaloue birds!" he muttered in exasperation.

We kids had learned years before that gillaloue birds were mythical birds of the lumber camps, the only place they ever took up residence. They laid square eggs, and were too intensely dumb to know how to build a nest to accommodate their purposes. Dad's inference, of course, was that the hired men sure didn't know anything about "building", either!

# 6

# THIRTY A MONTH AND BEANS

DAD NEVER HAD ANY TROUBLE GETTING HIRED
hands to work for him. He didn't need them in wintertime,
only through the planting season, the haying and harvesting
season.

Maybe one of the reasons he had no trouble getting
"harvest hands" was because of the reputation of Mother's
cooking—she owned culinary achievements that were a
legend in all neighborhoods around. Every single meal was
a sumptuous repast, starting right at breakfast time. Cooked
cereal usually, toast and eggs, cups and cups of excellent
coffee made in the big granite coffee pot. And always some
canned fruit or some delectable homemade jam from the
root cellar. Often there were buttermilk pancakes made with
buttermilk that had big gobs of sweet butter floating in it.

Mother definitely had a way with food. Her own way.
Take her raisin pie, for instance. It was made of inch-sized
seeded raisins, a couple cups of them simmered on the

Dad never had any trouble
getting hired hands to work for him.

back of the stove in half a saucepan of cold water (she didn't bother to measure), a cup of brown sugar and a big third, scant-half, cup of cider vinegar. It was thickened with corn starch or flour when all the raisins looked "swelled" enough, and the mixture was the right color. The mixture was allowed to cool and poured into an unbaked pie crust. It was always made "open faced" with no upper crust. And the last touch before it went into the oven of the Kalamazoo wood range was a generous sprinkling of nutmeg. Always, always, whole nutmeg was used, and ground with a tiny nutmeg grater. The grater was never used for anything except grinding nutmeg. Positively.

With raisin pie, then and now, it is customarily made with a double crust. Not Mother's. She always used only the bottom crust. And there'd be those beautiful, puffy, giant raisins gazing up at you, face to face. The vinegar and brown sugar and the sweetness of the raisins gave it a sweet-sour taste. The recipe made a big pie, and a thick one. The hired hands said it went right to the ribs for sustaining power.

Mother was a great consumer of buttermilk. Buttermilk biscuits, buttermilk Johnny cake, buttermilk pancakes, and soft molasses cookies made with buttermilk that stayed soft for a couple weeks. They were packed in gallon crocks and covered with an ironstone plate for a lid. Her big scalloped sugar cookies, too, were made with buttermilk.

She made apple dumplings, served with heavy sweet cream. And "Cottage pudding" with a pudding sauce also having that sweet-sour taste. Never, never have I successfully been able to duplicate that topping. It came out too sour, too pasty-pale, too dark, too something sadly wrong. The other girls in the family don't know the recipe either. Mother, it seems, just made it out of her head.

Her bread puddings were loaded with raisins, also served with heavy sweet cream, or the pudding sauce. Maybe the fact that the puddings were made from home-made bread gave them that special flavor.

Somehow, Mother knew the favorite dishes of each hired hand and they enjoyed the flattery of being remembered by seeing their favorite food on the table before them.

I cannot remember that Mother ever created a fluke in her baking. She had no beautiful cooking ware; her huge applesauce cakes and molasses cakes were usually baked in black "dripping pans" so big that one of them occupied the complete oven space. Beans were usually baked in small butter crocks, very slowly, and for hours and hours.

Looking back, it was truly amazing the patience those hired hands had with a bunch of bratty young'n's around. They played Checkers, Dominoes and Authors with us, and continually beat us. Maybe, they couldn't always read the names of the authors on the cards because of their inapt spelling ability, but they knew them all by their pictures. Once June, one of the twins, took some ink and colored the white whiskers of Henry Wadsworth Longfellow a jet black. And Jean, the other twin, put brown whiskers—long and luxuriant, on Edgar Allen Poe who had a face as smooth as a citron in Mother's garden. Even then, we couldn't win!

Every year just before the hired men came to work, we kids were given a thorough coaching by Dad. "None of your smart alecky shenanigans," he'd advise. He meant no showing off how good we could read and spell. And no showing off how well we knew our "Times tables" through the twelves.

One year at school we had a teacher who had us learn two new words each day. She said it was to "enrich your vocabulary." It is truly amazing how a vocabulary can take on surprising magnitude with two new words each day. Dad had a special message for a couple of us who doubled our quota of two words a day, and got enriched by four words a day. "No showin' off on some of them new words of yours," he advised with emphasis. And there'd be no correcting the hired man's grammar, or trying him out on a spelling lesson. "Just mind your little ole, very own business!" he cautioned.

Beulah and little H. B. liked the stint of learning four new words each day. We were both avid readers, and were reading eighth grade "stuff" when we were in the sixth grade and fourth grades respectively. Once H. B. used a word Beulah wasn't familiar with to date. She went tattling to Dad that Hazel had called her a name and she didn't know what it meant, but thought, maybe, it was a dirty word. Dad called me over to him, put his hand on my shoulder, and asked me what exactly had I said. I stuck out my breast bravely and hastily—and I didn't have any bust to expand, and said: "I can, too, spell it!" Blurted the spelling right out, pronto and correctly. Dad told Beulah I had spelled it right, used it correctly—so it could be my word anytime I wanted to use it. To this day, sisters in the family will inquire of each other: "Can you spell it?"

It was astonishing, downright awesome to us, the miscellaneous knowledge some of those hired men had. They knew the names of every tree in the creek flats, a giant dishpan gully with a creek running through it. Those flats probably contained a specimen of every tree native to the state of Michigan. They knew the names of all birds that came to the orchard, the fields, or the thickets of the creek flats. They knew where they wintered, and could tell what birds laid the eggs in a certain bird's nest. They liked the way Dad always cut the weeds along the fence rows with a scythe so the bob-whites' nests and the quails' nest would not be destroyed.

They knew many strange and wonderful things we kids didn't learn in school—things like bats can fly, but are not birds, but are mammals. They have fur, and they feed their babies milk. They said that bats slept during the daytime and did their flying after the sun sets. They said the expression "blind as a bat" was wrong, that bats really had good eyesight.

They knew that bats slept hanging upside down in a

hollow tree, or cracks in a building. Said the only dangerous ones were the vampire bats from South America—they lived on blood, and a bite from them could be dangerous. They knew that baby bears are born in winter, usually by twos. They were very tiny at birth and extremely helpless, and the mother bears were excellent mothers, and teachers, Very exacting teachers, and the cubs learned to mind. They said the expression "clumsy as a bear" was wrong, too. Maybe they might look clumsy walking on their hind legs, but they could run as fast as a pony, and climb a tree as fast as a squirrel.

Sometimes, it was downright disgusting all the knowledge some of those hired men had—like birds are warmblooded and have a normal temperature of 112 degrees, more warm-blooded than humans. They said the reason we didn't see birds migrating southward was because most of them flew at night and rested in the daytime. They got ready for their long flights by eating and eating a great deal. They said there were "four fly-ways" in the United States that the birds used—but most birds, including ducks, "took the Mississippi fly-way." Some northern birds preferred the Atlantic fly-way and took it year after year.

I can remember yet the dirty look Dad gave me, with his green eyes taking on an amber glaze, the time I asked a hired man how to spell "Mississippi." Inwardly, it was a trick of spite on my part. I was irritated because he had so much knowledge I wished I had. It was a lingering, devastating, dirty look Dad gave me, a staring, disgusted look. Then he said: "Why don't you go out and fetch in a pail of water?"

# 7

# PASS THE VITTLES, EUNICE

AND THERE WAS UNCLE HIRAM FROM MOTHER'S "side of the fence." Everyone called him "Hi" and it wasn't because of his longitude, for he only stood five feet and one or a couple inches tall.

Uncle DeLormey had always maintained that work was all for fools and horses. Uncle Hiram worked like a horse, worked like two horses—and that makes a team on anyone's farm. Uncle 'Lorm believed you had only one back, and that one had to last you a long time. Uncle Hi believed that bending and picking, and pitching and lifting was good for the spine—kept it strong and maneuverable. Kept one young, and kept you from getting "stove up" as you got older.

He jogged long before it was fashionable to jog. And he didn't jog in Bermuda shorts and a T-shirt. No siree, Robert! He jogged in the blue bib overalls he'd put on at getting-up-time. They were faded blue denim that weren't manufactured that color, but had achieved that shade from long hours under the scorching sun, and dozens of scrubbings on the washboard—hand-scrubbed with the faithful cleaning servant of the day, "Oak Leaf" soap.

There were patches on top of patches on those bib overalls, on the knees, and on the south end of them headed due north. No iron-on patches, mind you, no zig-zag stitching—but "hand-done" stitches as neat as embroidery work.

He jogged on the way to the barnyard to milk the cows, jogged back to the house for breakfast, jogged to the barn to harness the horses for the day's work.

He was known by neighbors and a host of relatives as "Money Bags." But no one could rightly say that Uncle Hiram was tight with a buck, he was just prudent. With ten children, he knew full well the value of the "Ole Oscar Mezulla," as he put it. He knew that regardless of how you stretched it, sliced it, spliced it—it just took a lot of it to go 'round.

Take in the matter of straw hats, he saved several dollars every summer. Other farmers bought their straw hats at the general store, but not Uncle Hi. His were hand-fashioned out of catalpa leaves. There was a catalpa tree growing down the lane that led from the road to the house. And the leaves on that catalpa tree were always 9-10 inches across, plus a stem as long as comes on a greenhouse rose. By using the stem for a darning needle he fashioned the leaves together, and got a hat out of it. It came well down over his forehead and covered his neck from the sunshine rigors.

He made it several thicknesses of leaves, and always claimed it was much cooler than a store-bought hat. Cows have a proclivity for eating straw hats, so Uncle Hi saved several dollars each summer. He'd make a catalpa hat first thing in the morning after breakfast, and it would last till noon when he'd make another one. On an extra hot scorching day, sometimes he would come to the house, mid-afternoon, grab a few catalpa leaves and fashion another chapeau. Always on the run. No pokin' along, no moseyin' along, always a well synchronized, syncopated jog.

The cows around his place never experienced the pleasure of tasting a straw hat. 'Twas like being a kid, and not knowing the taste of a baked Alaska pie till you were old enough to vote.

Uncle Hi's house was strictly utilitarian. No furbelows—like what-not shelves loaded with trinkets and gadgetry. His creed was if you couldn't use it, couldn't eat it, you just didn't need it! All as simple as that. His subtraction always made his addition look good. Save a bit here, and a bit there, and it all added up. Was really surprising what you could save in a year if you just learned to say "NO!" If a fast-talking salesman came around selling magazine subscriptions, or a photographer wanted to take pictures of those "darling, beautiful children," he could say "No!" with a negative ramification that would give a salesman a trauma that would last for at least a week.

He subscribed to a daily newspaper, took a couple of farm magazines, a needlecraft magazine for Aunt Eunice, and that was that! He reasoned that a thorough reading of the daily newspaper was a good education in itself. "Two and two make four, and four and four make eight," he used to say in his best addition by subtraction short-cut arithmetic.

Uncle Hiram's farm had a lot of low spots on it that required much draining by the laying of tile. Ditches had to be dug to make room for the tile. And it was said by neighbors and some covetous relatives that there was many a day when he didn't even take time off to come to the house at noon and eat his meal properly, seated around the family board with the rest of his family.

His wife, Eunice, prepared a basket, and took it to the field where he was working. The food in it was always something that would "carry well." Escalloped potatoes with slices of side pork baked on top, or maybe new potatoes and green peas fixed together with white sauce.

There'd be green onions and radishes from the garden, and always a gargantuan piece of pie—usually apple or raisin. And a pot of green tea. Uncle Hi would keep on keeping busy with the shovel, making a ditch for the tile burial.

Aunt Eunice would follow along the side of the ditch, and fork the food into Uncle Hiram's mouth as he worked along, without the shovel missing a scoopful. Neighbors who had seen the spectacle said it reminded them of a mother robin feeding worms to her young. Nope, no noon hour off for Uncle Hiram. He worked straight through the hottest part of the day, and had well-drained fields to show for it.

Aunt Eunice developed varicose veins at an early age. Neighbors said it was from having such a large family and having the young'un's so close together. But the relatives vowed it was from squatting along, ditch-side, shoveling food into Hiram's waiting mouth.

Anyway, Uncle Hi was always able to jog home for supper, and Aunt Eunice, varicose veins notwithstanding, raised ten kids who were healthy, industrious—and knew the full value of a buck, a quarter, a dime and a nickel. Soiled copper pennies were scoured by the youngest kids with vinegar and salt, and became beautiful filthy lucre.

Uncle Hiram was the first one around to own a pick-up truck, and the first one to own a "stake job." Always he paid "spot cash" for his purchases. There were no carrying charges ever added to his purchases. Never! He savored the savings of all investments he made. "A penny here, a penny there soon made a buck, and five bucks made a fin," he always reminded his family.

That stake job of his was one of his best investments, he always said. "With one of those babies, you're practically your own boss, and can pretty much write your own ticket," he'd say as he poured water from the sprinkling can into his thirsty radiator. He would take his own livestock to the market and cut out the middleman. He got more hep each week, it seemed, and maneuvered his goings and comings so he had a "pay load" each way. He'd contact the farmers for miles around and take orders for fertilizer, and thus have a "pay load" on the way coming home. He soon invested in a livestock truck and it was used for transporting livestock and chickens only, and the stake job was used for bringing back a load of peaches or other seasonal fruit for the housewives for miles and miles around. He would go directly to the orchards and contract for a full load for the next trip.

A good "picker-outer," he recognized good merchandise when he saw it. Nothing but the best for Uncle Hi. The housewives trusted his opinions better than they did their own. If he told them the peaches would be perfect, they would be 100 percent that way. No bruises, no spavins, no decayed ones. Not a bad peach in a bushel. The housewives would phone him at night (they always got Aunt Eunice in the daytime) and tell him that their bushel of peaches "dressed out" 22 quarts of canned fruit to the bushel, while the ones they got from the store just barely made up a scant 16 quarts. Uncle Hi would put his thumbs in his bib overall straps and remind them: "Ole Hi will never bring you a wilted flower, baby." If they called him and said they had a crateful of chickens for him to pick up, he'd ask if the chickens were blue-eyed or brown. The ladies loved it, and were always telling Aunt Eunice what a heck of a swell guy she had. Aunt Eunice left that one dangling in the atmosphere, always without corroboration.

For several months he had been bringing home day-old bread from his trips. Shucks! it was better when it had been around in the world and had a day's growth on its back. Or take bread 3-4 days old, it was still better. And at a dozen loaves for a dollar, one couldn't go far wrong. Made better toast that was for sure. Bread a week old was the best of all—better for milk toast, bread pudding, chicken stuffin' or most anything. His marketing junkets had "opened up a whole new can of worms" for him. He was always picking up some new lingo in the market places, and took on a language entirely different than the farmers around him.

Uncle Hi really hit pay dirt when he hit onto the idea of feeding the vintaged bread to his feeder cattle. He had noticed that when he fed the antiquated bread to his hogs, that the young livestock also had a hankering for it, so he connived the idea of bringing home enough for them, too. He'd drive the truck right out into the field where the livestock was feeding on green grass, whip out his jackknife from the special jackknife pocket in his bib overalls, and slit the waxed paper off the loaves of bread, and toss it to the impatient livestock. The cattle would forsake the greenest grass and come running for the "staff of life." He noted early in his delivery program that the cattle had a special liking for the cracked wheat variety and the darker breads. Uncle Hi always had his feeder cattle ready for market weeks and weeks before any of his neighbors around him.

"Nothing like using the old gourd," he'd say, and point to the small head atop his 140-pound chassis—the same head that had worn out dozens of catalpa leaf hats in its time. If Uncle Hi didn't "laugh all the way to the bank," he certainly laughed when he got there. He could have taught most of them there a thing or a couple about investments, and certainly didn't need any of their lendings. He was a self-made , all sufficient man, who liked himself for his own astuteness, and promised never to let himself down. He used to say it would be a cold day in January, February, March or April when any loan company would get his name on a piece of paper. Somehow, he never mentioned whether it could happen in November or December, or not. Once, one of the relatives heard Aunt Eunice break in with the delayed observation: "Who could live so long?"

He never flubbed on a financial maneuver; he believed in positive thinking long before it was acknowledged. The light of his world dimmed, however, the day he went to make a pickup of out-dated bread, and was told it would no longer be available for livestock feeding. He had to go home and disappoint the pampered livestock and tell Aunt Eunice. He'd told her important things like that before, and her stock answer had always been: "Well, what now, Ebenezer?"

# 8

# MONEY ISN'T EVERYTHING

NO NETTLES SCALED THE GARDEN WALL; NO
ragweed, pigweed, mullein weed, burdock or wild mustard,
claimed seniority rights along the garden fence row.

It was Mother's garden, flower and vegetable—extraordinary and magnificent. There are no Marquis of Queens-
bury rules in a flower garden. And our mother could coax
more ringside suspense out of a dime package of seeds
than anyone I had ever known. Sober-faced pansies, that
looked like innocent choir boys in a cathedral loft, took
their corners; galloping hollyhocks, like song and dance
guys in a soft shoe act, took their corners; sweet peas hung
tenaciously to the ropes—and only Luther Burbank himself
could have picked a winner.

As a youngster, I took the high-amperage beauty of
Mother's flower garden pretty much for granted, seemed
like it was always there. It was always present and ac-
counted for as soon as the gargantuan snowdrifts sagged

along the fence rows, and Maw Nature with sometimes strident mutterings set about her annual house-cleaning. With her efficient broom, the March wind, she swept every nook and cranny. And with barrels and buckets filled with April showers, she washed the face of all Creation.

But Mother's flowers were always there waiting—like Ole Cherry, the "bell cow," waiting at the pasture bars, come summer sundown. It was one of those things you just naturally expected and took for granted, one of the big, little things in life.

I have picked huge velvety pansies from her garden during days of "woodpecker thaws" of a severe northern Michigan winter. Through their straw mulching, they double-dared the elements and came out of their boudoirs, replete in purple velvet—and wearing it as casually as a belle of the Klondike wore her hourglass velvet in the cold, gold days of the Alaskan "pay dirt."

But the summer fiasco of blooms is what put you agog, aghast, astern and avast. You plumb forgot about the pot of gold at the end of the rainbow, or any of its drippings.

It wasn't a floral shindig that was a Buffalo Bill show, an Irish wake with a little soupcon of a World Series' game, a John Glenn day and a Lithuanian wedding all put together. It was a prodigious beauty, yet in an orderly planned sort of way. No rambunctious nasturtiums stole the show from dainty sweet alyssums nor castor bean bushes confiscate the beauty of her yellow rose bushes.

Not till I was a grown adult and became interested in photography did it dawn on my highly-astigmated scrawny mind the why and wherefore of the plural beauty of Mother's flower garden. Then, I realized why passersby had always slowed up their cars or stopped completely in front of the Home Place, while they gazed, beheld—and probably long remembered.

The study of photography and its attending problems of composition, balance and light, made me realize exactly why Mother's flower garden perennially clicked and rang the bell.

I doubt very much that Mother in her youth ever studied art and learned the intrinsic value of proper balance and composition. But she had something better—a natural, in-born sense of those values. She never studied landscaping but owned something definitely much better, one of the greenest green thumbs in the world. She probably didn't know, or even guess, that the manufacturing process of green cells in plants is known by the highpower monicker of "photosynthesis." But a growing plant just stretched and grew right out of its chlorophyll pants and shirt to win her favors.

She didn't have too much Oscar Mezulla, the old pay-ola, to spend on things that couldn't go on the table or be packed in lunch pails, such as delphinium roots. Instead, she knew first-hand the thrill of planting the seeds, and a couple summers later watch the humming birds hold their convention in her delphinium stockade. And if they got gaga and pixilated from the nectar, they always came back for more. Great convention-goers, those humming birds, and they really passed the word around.

The awesome problem of a utilitarian structure like a woodshed built too close to the house didn't deter Mother's magic green fingers or fertile imagination. She planted castor beans against the weathered boards and Mexican firebush in the foreground. And the color effect was so beautiful till frost claimed it—you plumb forgot the wood—shed.

Seemed like that woodshed was always getting a break. It was just lucky to have been born homely. Some years there'd be hollyhocks doing a calathumpian parade along its walls—great towering blue-black and rose-red ones, doubles and singles, that seemed to enhance the rough gray timbers. One year she planted giant cosmos, and they grew from short pants to long ones and kept right on gallivanting. They blossomed with reckless abandon, and oncoming

75

frosts found them loaded with hundreds and hundreds of buds still in their knapsacks. So reluctant was Mother to have the frost ravage them that she dug up half a dozen plants with generous wedges of earth clinging to their roots, and put them in wooden pails. Two of them were brought to the kitchen and the rest went to the woodshed. They were the bloomingest bloomin' flowers I ever did see! They blossomed till Christmas.

Sweet clover was planted around the windmill, and morning glories or moonflowers alternately did annual push-ups over the smokehouse. When she planted ruffled petunias, they were really ruffled, like the frills on a Gibson girl. She grew ostrich-feather asters with more furbelows on them than a dozen surreys, all with fringe on top. And she wanted her garden to smell, to please the sense of smell as well as sense of sight. So spicy pinks, mignonettes and fragrant heliotropes were among the flowers bound to be present.

. . . No, a thousand times no, it can never be said that daughter Hazel inherited the maternal green thumb. Just a pale, pasty, off-shade nile green thumb. Probably the one appendage of heritage that has been most treasureable has been the appreciation of the big, little things in life.

. . . So far, I've never earned a million dollars . . . and so far, I've never known the pain of having it to lose. I'm glad that as a kid I ran up a lot of mileage, following the freshly-plowed furrows as Dad prepared his fields for the planting season. The sustaining, bucolic memories of youth "last" a long time. Memories like those are remarkably "good keepers."

A horse-lover deluxe, Dad's well-fed horses, filled with oats and guile, were stopped every few rounds of the fields to rest. High-rumped and cadaverous, high-spirited as firecrackers, those horses didn't need a rest any more than the March of Time needs a wristwatch.

Time out to give the horses a "five" and we'd sit down on the stubble ground or on the rail fence and talk. Maybe talk about the big elms by the bridge, towering elms that had been scouted, labeled and ticketed before they reached the majors. We'd eat a McIntosh apple apiece, and he'd point out the chevrons of wild geese heading southward or a bob-white hollering from the fence corner. Maybe he'd sing a couple verses of a shantyboy ditty, like "The Jam on Garry's Rock," or try me out on some geography or hard spelling like "Massachusetts" or "Tennessee."

He'd toy with a handful of mellow loam picked up from the open furrow, and sift it affectionately between his fingers. Seemed everytime he plowed, he did a lot of dirt-sifting through his fingers—always said he could think better with nice, earthy dirt getting massaged in his hands. He'd talk about goldenrods 'long the fence row, cat-tails in the swamp—and somehow make you like them, too. He used to say that a love of the outdoors was something a bankroll couldn't buy. Why, great gallopin' grasshoppers! you could own a million bucks and if you didn't enjoy things like a bob-white sittin' on a rail fence, or a sight like Ole Cherry bringing the cows home through the pasture lane, you were still "hard up" in the things that really counted. Shucks, I'gollys! the little things were sometimes the BIG things in life . . . and didn't I think so, too?

. . . I used to think that Ole Cherry, our "bell cow," was the smartest bovine that ever wore a locket. She was a mental giant, that cow! She looked after the other cows like a Leghorn hen with twenty chicks. To her, year after year, was accorded the honor and voluble responsibility of wearing the cowbell.

When the sun reached a certain position in the sky—say 38-39-40 degrees above the horizon, Ole Cherry brought her charges up to the pasture bars. When the sky looked poutish and rainy, she headed them for the creek flats where the dense underbrush provided the protection of a model dairy barn. All brains and all milk, that cow.

I've seen her standing on the brow of a hill shifting her cud with the nonchalance of a veteran scrap-tobacco chew-

Dad's horses were always filled
with oats and guile.

er. Round and round, to and fro, went the regurgitated after-dinner clover mint in her mouth—and all the time she looked off in the distance, big-eyed and thinky-like. I used to wonder what she was thinking about, if anything. A ponderous look like that on a kid's face in the schoolroom usually brought the admonition to "Get with it, sleepy!"

One time I asked Dad what he thought Ole Cherry was thinking about, and he said she looked that way because she was contented, that she did a good day's work and did it every day in the week. Said she was a dern good cow, and KNEW she was good. And this automatically gave her the privilege of looking any way she wanted to look—down her nose, off in the distance, or pat herself on the back—if she thought she could.

## 9

# SWEET RINGING BELL
# OF OLE CHERRY

CAME THE EVENING, THE AFTER-SUPPER PART
of the evening, when the cows were not waiting at the
pasture bars to be milked. They were not there, nor could
Ole Cherry—the bell cow, be seen bringing them down the
last turn in the lane toward home. Cherry, the head moo-
moo, had at last, made a boo-boo. She just hadn't brought
the cows home on time. She had goofed for the first time in
her life. For years and years she had never even been
tardy; she had always taken her "bell cow" obligations
seriously.

Mother was the first one to notice that the cows weren't
home, and sent me scampering to hurry them up. She said
they were probably headed home already and I'd probably
meet them. Said she thought the dark gray sky overhead,
without sunlight, had confused Cherry and she hadn't
realized how late it was. There were ominous rolls of

thunder, foretelling an approaching storm, and her reason sounded sensible.

Through the three turns in the lane I didn't find them coming home. I crossed the creek on the big log we always used to go to the pasture beyond the creek flats. The cows hadn't budged from the pasture but were laying down chewing their cuds, without any pretense of going anywhere. Ole Cherry was not with them which was probably the reason they hadn't come home. Without her, they sure didn't know their geography. All their lives they'd "been pickin' her brains" 'it suddenly occurred to me. Without her, they were just milk manufacturers and didn't know the pasture from the barnyard—it was very obvious she had to do their thinking for them.

I looked and looked through the creek flats and could not find her anywhere. There wasn't the slightest tinkle of her melodic bell, a copper resonant bell that could be heard a great distance away. It occurred to me that possibly she had broken through the fence and had gotten out, and automatically the question answered itself. No cow would ever get through one of Dad's well-built fences. Anywhere. Anytime. It was an insured impossibility.

The sky was getting darker; the woods in the creek flats were getting darker; the rolling thunder was getting noisier, and closer. I wanted desperately to be out of there, but thought I must find Ole Cherry. Maybe she had a broken leg . . . Did cows ever have heart attacks? . . . Maybe the strap on her bell had broken and the bell was lost. No wonder it wasn't ringing! . . . Maybe she had just gotten tired of shepherding the other cows and tired of being a continual chaperon, and was going to show 'em and stay completely away from the tag-a-longs. Mosquitoes were getting terrible in the humid underbrush, and I did wish Mother hadn't sent me alone.

Just when my thoughts were getting at a low-down melancholy ebb, I came upon Ole Cherry. She let out a slight mooing sound when she saw me. She raised her head slightly from the ground, and the copper bell about her neck gave a subdued clang. She mooed again, and it wasn't a happy sound. One look—one startled, unbelievable look, told me she was having a calf. It was being born right that minute, and half of it seemed to already be there, right there, on the floor of the creek flats.

I left real quickly to run home to tell Dad. I crossed the log in the creek; I ran through the three turns in the lane. It seemed a small forever getting home. The hired man, Bob Webster, saw me coming as fast as a kid could run, and came to meet me. He didn't stop to tell Dad. He took off down the lane, and I was amazed at how fast he could run. It didn't occur to me that any grown-up man could run that fast unless he was a ball player. I never did catch up with him until I saw him standing by Cherry's side. The calf had already been born when he reached her and was standing, wobble-legged, getting its first meal. Ole Cherry was stretching her neck to get back licking her youngster, and once again her copper bell was giving out a nice melody.

The hired man took his blue chambray shirt off and wrapped it securely around the wobbly calf. He headed for the creek, with the log across it for a bridge. But he didn't bother to take the log; he didn't bother to take off his shoes and sox or roll up the legs of his blue bib overalls— he splashed right through the creek, with Ole Cherry mooing at his heels. He carried the calf up the steep side of the gully; he was breathless and soaking wet with sweat. It was rolling down his forehead and into his eyes; the beads of sweat rolling down his face and neck were as big as the "clearies" we kids used in playing marbles.

He sat down to rest at the top of the gully, and Ole Cherry got back to licking her youngster. He rested briefly, and again took up his cargo. I couldn't figure what all his haste was about at this point. Cherry had been found; she had her family with her, but he ran most of the way home with the calf in his arms wrapped tenderly in the shirt off his back.

When we arrived home, it was long past milking time. Dad came running; Mother came running; the other kids came running and started petting the new calf. Mother stopped them abruptly and told them, not too sweetly, that they knew better than to be petting a new calf. Some new mother cows didn't think too much of the idea.

Dad put her in the cow stable along with her calf so she'd be alone to enjoy her post motherhood, and went to the horse stable and brought a blanket and put it over Cherry's back. It looked like a silly thing to do on a hot sticky night but I was sure Dad knew what he was doing. He always knew, always.

We all went into the house, and from the kitchen we would hear the happy ringing of Ole Cherry's bell. That smart cow had done it again! The other cows hadn't helped her any. Shucks! They couldn't even find their own way home.

Perhaps the incident of seeing Ole Cherry giving birth to a calf in the woodland thickets had something to do with my life-long aversion for veal in any form. Ah! sweet memory of veal—I liked you better on the hoof wrapped around the body of a young calf, a very young calf, just being weaned from its mother. A kid remembers things like putting a hand down in a bucket of warm milk, freshly siphoned from a cow—and nudging your head gently down into the bucket, and you nursed and tugged on the fingers, and gulped down the fresh warm milk and thought you were at your mother's dairy bar. I could never, NEVER, eat you.

Perhaps the fact that we girls always owned and coddled pet lambs as kids on the farm, likewise, gave us all an aversion for lamb chops, leg of lamb, lamb roasts and the rest. It was not a temporary childhood dislike of the product involved—but a deeply-imbedded, enduring aversion that has remained through the years.

I can remember yet the twins, the pretty ones in the

family, and their pet lambs. They had little red rocking chairs, exactly alike, and would rock their lambs like crazy, and at times even get carried away and sing to them in their third grade sopranos. The lambs didn't tag them to school, like Mary's did in the book, but they had to be locked in the woodshed so they'd stay home.

Dad always tried to dissuade us kids from getting too attached to our pet lambs because, he always explained to us in detail, they would have to be sold come fall, just like the rest of the lambs. They just couldn't be kept. On the morning of the day he took them to market, to go bye-bye on the little narrow-gauge train, he always told us about it before we left for school. He didn't want us coming home and finding the lambs missing.

A girl at school, Edna Garrett, whose folks owned the farm right next to the schoolhouse, always had many pet lambs every spring. It seemed that the ewes at the Garrett place were always having twins, or sometimes triplets. When those extra dividends came along on the farm, it usually meant some of them have to be bottle-fed. It takes a certain tenderized, patient disposition like Edna had or our sister Amy, to bottle-feed a squirming hungry lamb. Sometimes through the years I have found myself wondering if Edna received any lasting "hangups" about lamb as a protein nutrient.

Edna, also, had a pet crow that was spoiled beyond apology. It often lit on her shoulders and had free transportation anytime she ventured out the door. Edna always said the crow could speak many words very distinctly, and many of the school kids vouched for the truth of her statement. I'm sure her exploitation of the crow was entirely correct, even though, personally, it never chose to verbalize when I was around. Probably didn't want to be crowing about the smart crow he really was.

That bird continually committed larceny and hid all evidence. He would pluck clothespins off a line loaded with clean laundry and the clothespins would never be found

85

Dad always warned us kids
not to get too attached to the lambs—
some day they'd have to be sold.

again. He liked bright objects like beads and earrings, hair ribbons and barrettes; he liked the buttons on a man's shirt; he liked the red comb on the barnyard rooster. He'd light on a cow's back and start scratching like a mother robin after a warm rain. Mrs. Garrett always said he was looking for ticks and always knew exactly which cow owned the most of his delectables.

It is often said that a crow will not talk unless his tongue is split. I am very sure the Garrett crow never underwent such surgery. However, he did have his wings clipped a little to keep him from flying too far away.

Edna's crow always sounded like a wonderful pet to own. Not many people are blessed with the staunch companionship of a pet crow. However, it is truly amazing how much crow is consumed annually in the United States. The average man consumes a generous quotient of it daily. It's always verbal, however, and definitely without a protein content.

## 10

# CEDAR SWAMP DAYS

EACH WINTER DAD WENT INTO THE CEDAR swamp to "get out" the fence posts he would need the following summer. He had the perimeter of the farm fenced with woven wire fencing. His pride and joy, a 30-acre field in one unbroken area, without a stump or visible stone, was fenced on two sides with woven wire, and the long lane, with three turns in it, had the beautiful rail fencing.

The long stretch of the field bordering the creek flats had barbed wire fencing. None of the sissy barbed wire such as is sold under that name today, made of light-weight wire with three tiny prongs. Dad's barbed wire was the old-fashioned kind that really meant business. It was made of heavy-gauge wire, and the barbs were placed close together along the wire. The barbs were four-pronged and each prong about an inch long. It was the kind of barbed wire that fenced the West in the long ago, the barrier that announced to the open range that civilization had come to the land. It meant the end of the wild freedom of the West.

Photo by H. Girard

Dad had a rail fence
down the long lane to the pasture gully.

A year or so ago, I noted an ad in a western magazine calling attention to barbed wire as a "conversation piece" antique. The price was one dollar per foot, containing a "setting" of the old ranch-style 4-pronged barbs. Or for three dollars, it could be bought in a rustic frame.

Today, 50 years and more later, the barbed wire fencing on the "Home Place" still endures. No leaning over of the fence posts; they're standing erectly and proudly, as they have a just right to do. The cedar posts were "put down deep" and the bottoms of them well treated with creosote before being placed.

Dad usually made his junkets to the cedar swamps on Saturdays. That way, one of the kids could go along and hold the reins of the skittish horses while he worked. If a jackrabbit in the woods had made a quick jump ahead of them, they probably would have been involved in another runaway and been over the county line before they stopped. Usually, it was Beulah or H. B. he took along for the sentry duty. He couldn't take one of the twins without taking both of them. And their giggling antics would have had the horses running through two counties.

Once Dad found a squirrel's nest in a hollow tree. He came back to the sleigh to hold the horses' reins so I could take a look at the baby squirrels. He cautioned me not to touch them. He need not have worried. I thought they looked terrible—without fur, eyes closed, and certainly not looking anything like squirrels. I even wished I hadn't looked at all.

The mother moved off a short distance and acted hysterical. She chattered and scolded, sputtered and stomped her feet, and went into a monologue of seething rage. It occurred to me she sure, sure had one awful temper, and was the mother of some terribly homely kids.

Next week, and the week after, they still had their eyes closed and I told Dad I thought they were blind, all four of them. He explained that baby squirrels did not open their eyes for a month. Dad was right. It was a month at least

91

before their eyes opened, and by the time they moved into the sunlight, they were fully clothed and made up for the time they were sightless. They romped like school kids "let out at recess."

Dad said squirrels usually galloped up a tree, but came down much more cautiously. He said they were great planters of trees without knowing it because they sometimes forgot where they had hidden their cache of nuts, seeds, fruit and such. They used so many places for storage—like underground, next to logs and rocks, and holes in trees, they just forgot where they'd hidden all their goodies. Women, sometimes, have been found guilty of the same maneuver.

Often late in winter would come a day of "woodpecker thaws" in the woods. From all directions would come a sound of pecking, petulous woodpeckers. They'd claim a heyday and come forth to make tryst with fair weather. The forest corridors would echo with their staccato hammering, a rhythmic rat-a-tat-tat that never let up.

They'd stand with their powerful feet made with special equipment for the task at hand—viciously strong claws, with two toes extending forward and two toes backward, and proceed to light out for calories. They were like starving lumberjacks who thrust their calked boots into the rough-hewn timbers of the chuckhouse floor. The jacks would brace their feet with good anchorage, and long-arm it for vittles across the family board. It was the same exact stance the woodpeckers used, and for the same purpose.

Some entomologists claim that woodpeckers, those little saviours of our national resources, can even hear the larvae and insects inside the tree bark getting drunk on tree ale. Perhaps. You'll see 'em saluting "Attention!" and all at once look like they've heard a dinner gong. You know what I mean—you'll see the same expression on a man's face about three times a day, sort of a "When do we eat?" look. You can get the very same identical effect from tapping very gently the nest of some very young robins.

Each time Dad went to the cedar swamp he took along some clover hay and cracked corn to feed the white-tailed deer in the swamp. He always deposited the hay and corn quite a distance from the sleigh so the horses wouldn't be perturbed by the company.

At first the deer stood back a considerable distance and watched, big-eyed and thinky. Slowly, one by one, they came stealthily toward the hay. They nibbled slowly as if to make it last a long time. There were a dozen in the herd, but only three of them participated in the first banquet. The others stood back, big-eyed and suspicious.

Dad once looked at their dainty cloven-hoofed tracks made by a mature deer and said half-aloud, like he was thinking deeply: "Who could eat a grown animal that makes a delicate, tiny track like that?" I cannot remember Dad ever hunting . . . cannot remember him ever "shouldering a gun." Rabbit, too, was off his edible list always, said it would be too much like eating our shepherd dog, Prince.

He used to tell about the lean, lean years he and Mother had known when they first broke the virgin land, and cultivated the dense wilderness about them to a beautiful farm. "Lean years, they sure were!" He'd say with emphasis. Yet somehow, somehow, they always managed to have three meals a day: "Oatmeal, cornmeal, and miss a meal," he remembered with desperation.

As kids growing up, we didn't have pheasant under glass, or pheasant anything. No partridge, or wild ducks which were plentiful in nearby marshes and lakes.

My brother, George, always went hunting every fall, went with some railroad buddies from Jackson, and they usually went to Michigan's Upper Peninsula. One fall he didn't go to the U. P. but went hunting in the area within walking distance from the Home Place. Crack marksman that he was, he did indeed get his deer, and a big one. And then he didn't know what to do with it. It was an autumn of unduly warm weather, and there were no freezing facilities around. It was too warm, much too warm, for the venison to be frozen outdoors, and Dad wouldn't permit it on the table. George couldn't even freeze a few pieces to take back home with him. Most of it was given to friends and neighbors nearby.

But Mother kept a few pieces of it strictly on the Q. T. and with the assistance of Northern Spy apples, raisins, suet, brown sugar, spices and a wee bit of cider vinegar converted it into mincemeat. Dad for years had always eaten pie for breakfast, a carry-over from his lumberjack days of eating in the chuckhouse. Did we have mincemeat pie! We had it for breakfast; the kids had it in their lunch pails; we had giant wedges of it for supper. We kids "went easy" on the consumption of potatoes, bread and butter and the rest of the food on the supper table to leave room for second helpings of mincemeat pie.

Often Mother would inveigle Dad into the second healthy helping of pie for breakfast, and the same generosity prevailed at supper, washed down with the second and third cups of green tea. The tea was made with green tea siftings, better known as "tea dust." Dad always told Mother she had really outdone herself in concocting that mincemeat—said she really had given it just the right "Johannah touch."

Not until the big crocks of venison mincemeat were completely gone did Mother enlighten the family that they had been eating mincemeat made from George's deer. Dad blew his top; he verbally and physically almost raised the roof of the stable. Shucks! he almost blew the roof of the outdoors off, starting right at the back door.

There was a cold war on. A cold, cold war. Dad wasn't talking to Mother and she wasn't talking back. At first, Dad blamed the kids because they hadn't told him anything. Fact was, the kids hadn't known the vital ingredients of the mincemeat either. We were "off the hook" and Mother had to assume the blame. Solo, all by herself.

Mother took to eating her meals in the kitchen; Dad and the kids ate at the long, oblong oak table in the dining room. Mother quit making Dad's favorite buttermilk biscuits. No more morning pancakes; no more applesauce cake; no more fat sugar cookies. Mother went on a binge of cooking pork liver—we'd have it for breakfast, and again for supper. Dad said that porker must have had a liver as big as a washtub.

Mother moved her little rocking chair to the kitchen, and in the evenings after supper would carry on with her knitting and darning. Messages were passed back and forth between them via kid messengers. Mother would have one of the kids tell Dad thus and so, and Dad would employ the same messenger service. We kids would go to school and ponder all day about the cold, cold war at home. Words between them were totally non-existent when we were home, so we wondered what system of communication they used when we were at school.

Meals weren't so flavorable during the wordless siege of the household. It was mostly meat and potatoes, and things from the root cellar. Turnips appeared often on the menu. (Dad hated turnips.) We had creamed cabbage, baked cabbage, and fried cabbage. (Dad always said that cabbage gave him the heartburn.) The only thing that really truly hit the spot was the limitless supply of homemade jam. Mother had always "turned out" wonderful homemade bread. Somehow, suddenly the burned black crust was an integral part of the loaf. Mother said the wood was "burning flashy" and she just couldn't control the oven.

Dad stayed in the horse stable more and more, currying and currying the horses. The hips on those horses had a sheen on them like the patent leather shoes that we kids wore for "good." We always had shoes for "good" and dresses for "good." He'd read the *Michigan Farmer* and the *Farm Journal* over and over again. We got the *Detroit Journal* each day in the mail, by courtesy of the R. F. D. They were currently having a contest for limerick writing. They gave a dollar each day for the best limerick published, and five dollars for the best limerick published during the week, and twenty-five dollars for the best one submitted through the month. Dad submitted an offering that went like this:

> "An old lady once hit her thumb with a hammer
> She murmured out something that sounded like 'Da-da-dammer!'
> The folks who were there
> Thought she was learning to swear
> Never before had they heard the old lady stammer."

Dad's contribution copped the daily prize, the weekly prize, and the best limerick-of-the-month prize. He had netted $31.00 for his brief stint of work. Subsequent brain children were accepted and published, and Mother referred to him smilingly as "The Limerick Kid."

Poetry was an easy task for Dad. It rolled off the end of his penny cedar lead pencil without an effort. One of his renditions written during the cold war ended this way:

> ". . . And gladly she'll wear it though madly we tear it
> That old ragged wrapper my housekeeper wore."

That's all I remember of that particular poem but it certainly didn't lend anything toward a truce overture.

One afternoon when we kids got home from school, we found Dad and Mother both sitting in the kitchen. The oven door of the Kalamazoo wood range was wide open and hot breaths of heat were pouring forth. Mother was sitting in her little rocking chair, pulled up close to the oven. Dad was sitting in a red kitchen chair, with his knees practically in the oven. Each of them was holding a baby lamb in their arms, and feeding the lambs warm milk from nursing bottles, replete with nipples. Mother was holding a white lamb, and Dad was holding a bleating little black one. The ewe had abandoned the black one at birth, and while she was about it she decided she didn't want the white one either. She had definitely abandoned both of them, and it was up to Dad and Mother to bring up some more family.

Mother had the gray granite coffee pot on the back of the stove and had just broken a raw egg into the coffee, and dropped in the egg shells after it—the exact way that Dad liked it. He liked his coffee with a robust, full-bodied flavor, strong enough to take the barnacles off the Queen Mary. It was a friendly kind of coffee that made conversation easy.

## 11

# I'VE GOT MY YESTERDAYS

DAD USED TO TELL US KIDS OF AN AUNT OF HIS who married a light-keeper. In her youth, great-Aunt Lucinda had been a schoolma'am, a very pretty schoolma'am with gray-green eyes the color of ash buds in the front of March. She retired from teaching at the ripe old age of 36, and bought a little cottage with a white picket fence around an abundant garden.

The neighbors referred to her as "the old maid down the way." But great-Aunt 'Cindy, it seemed, never minded. She kept right on being adept at minding her own business, doing fancywork and tending her geraniums and begonias that blossomed by the dozens in her bright shuttered windows. Neighbors said she could put an old stick in the ground and it would blossom in a couple weeks. The magic and love of growing things seemed born in her finger tips. Thoreau and Luther Burbank would have loved her.

But suddenly, and very unexpectedly, great-Aunt 'Cindy

married a light-keeper who tended a light on some rock-bound forsaken spot along our Atlantic seaboard. Neighbors said she ought to know what she was doing. "Pity sakes!" and "Sakes alive!" she certainly was old enough.

She sold her little cottage with its white picket fence around it and all the lush growing things everywhere, and went to the lighthouse to live, taking several of her choice geraniums and begonias with her.

But the salt mist oozed in through the scanty windows; the sunshine was scarce, and one by one great-Aunt 'Cindy tossed the skeletons of her beloved plants to the rocks below the lighthouse windows. Each time she went ashore, she came back loaded with plants, mostly geraniums—red ones, salmon ones, doubles and singles. But they, too, didn't like the environment and soon joined the corpses of their predecessors on the rocks. More and more she missed the little cottage with the lilac tree at the back door where she used to hang her dishcloth to "air." She missed the quiet, ordinary things like dew in the early morning, and moist earthy smells after a warm rain, and vesper songs from the orchard at eventide.

After six months in the lighthouse, great-Aunt 'Cindy shuffled off this mortal coil. The light of the world, the light of her world, had gone out when the pleasure of growing things was taken from her life. Like the geraniums and begonias, she needed sunlight and open spaces, and terra firma underfoot—without salt.

\*　　\*　　\*

A few summers ago in "the Thumb" of Michigan, down a lonely country road, I saw a little girl of 9-10 years sitting by the fence of a large wheat field.

Said she often came out there before the wheat was cut, just to sit and watch it. Said she liked the wind blowing through its yellow heads, and the sun making it prettier every day. . . Didn't I think it was pretty, too?

Photo by H. Girard

"Can the camera really put the clouds in
and show the wind blowin' the wheat?"

She thought it was one of the prettiest things she knew, especially with wooly clouds in the sky, and the wind blowing the wheat. . . Everyone in the world probably ate wheat somehow or other, she said, and wondered if they knew how pretty wheat could really be. Said she could even remember how it looked in the wintertime when there were several inches of snow on the ground, didn't ever want to forget how pretty wheat was before it was cut.

And please, could she look through the camera and see how it looked. . . And could the camera really put the clouds in, and show the wind blowing the wheat?

Bless her little girl heart! I feel sure that as the seasons pass into years—and lambs in the meadows tell us that another spring has come, and cat-tails and goldenrods with their shafts and plumes against the sky announce that autumn has rolled around again, and Indian summer nudges winter—and she no longer is a little girl but woman-grown, I feel so very sure she will always remember her childhood love of ripening wheat.

Possibly she may not have much folding money, the elusive old Oscar Mezulla. But she'll be a rich woman with the greatest wealth of all—a full, cherishable love of the big, little things in life. And great, ringing bell of Ole Cherry, the world's her pocketbook!

\*　　\*　　\*

I remember the hired men coming in from the fields on a scorchin' hot day and headin' for the root cellar before washing up for a meal. Mother always kept large crocks of fresh buttermilk on the earthen floor of the roothouse. There were always beads of butter floating through the buttermilk, and the buttermilk had the same cold coldness of water freshly siphoned from the pump.

The hired men drank and drank, and drank, with the same rapt enthusiasm they drank the cold water from the jugs out in the fields. They drank the buttermilk, like next

Bless her little girl heart! . . .
When she no longer is a little girl
but woman-grown, she will always remember
her love of ripening wheat.

week there wouldn't be any. And that was pretty silly thinking—it was like guessing there wouldn't be any water flowing in the creek next week; like guessing there wouldn't be any water in Uncle 'Lorm's old oaken bucket when he brought it topside. Worse than that, it was like imagining there wouldn't be any milk pouring out the milk taps of the Jersey cows.

Mother always told us kids not to drink too much "of that awful cold, cold water" all at once on a hot day, said we might get terrible stomach cramps from it. Mother never cautioned the hired men about drinking too much cold buttermilk—guess she thought they were big boys now, and certainly old enough to know a cramp from a hiccup. It never seemed to spoil their meals any. Their appetites were always honed to a fine edge, with power, vigor and expectancy behind them.

They'd eat and eat—like next week the cupboards would all be bare, Mother would have two broken arms, and the yakity, laughing kids couldn't possibly put any vittles on the table. They thought crazy, those hired men, and drank and drank, and ate and ate, like "Babe" Bunyan—Paul's blue ox.

*       *       *

There was an Indian family who lived in our particular area. In summer they picked huckleberries and sold them. Mother always bought some from them even though she had a houseful of huckleberry pickers. They made beautiful baskets, and Mother probably owned one of each kind they made: clothesbaskets, laundry baskets, hand baskets like Little Red Riding Hood carried on the trip to her grandmother's; there were sweet grass baskets in all shapes and sizes. They were everywhere around the house. The sweet grass baskets smelled delightful for years and years.

Four of the Indian children went to our school, and all of them had Biblical names: Jacob, Eli, Samuel and Ruth.

Photo by H. Girard

I haven't much folding money
but I'm rich in the memories of yesterdays.

Each day in their lunch pails they would have smoked brook trout and canned huckleberries. The trout looked elegant, huge in size, and had a tantalizing smell that devastated the other kids to desperation with their egg and pork sandwiches, and even the heavenly homemade jam sandwiches. Occasionally the Indian youngsters would swap with the other kids in school—a trout for a whopping big Northern Spy apple, a trout for an orange or a piece of apple pie, or a trout for two Russet apples. But the Indian kids usually preferred their own fare. And why not? Those brook trout, ten or twelve inches long, were truly a gastronomic treat in the dead of winter, smoked to a beautiful tawny brown on the outside and the interior a delightful salmon pink.

One year we had a teacher who had had extensive Normal School training. She taught us how to frame pictures from calendars that had been discarded. Just cover the lovely picture with glass, put in a cardboard backing, bind it all around with paper mache tape. She had acquired the art of basket-weaving along with her other handicraft acquisitions. The Indian kids didn't think too much of her basket-weaving prowess. And besides, she bought the makings for the baskets already prepared—it seemed to the Indians it was a "cheating way" to be making baskets.

Those Indian children were always impeccably clean, and the other kids at school were delighted to have them in their games. It was true integration without deviation of thought. It was complete integration before the word was thought about. It was the height of esteem to be playing "The farmer's in the dell" and be chosen as the wife of the Indian farmer. H. B. of the fiery red hair loved to be chosen as the wife—the other kids labeled her "Pretty Red Wing" when she was chosen. Poor kid, it was the only time in her life that anyone, ANYONE, ever called her "pretty."

Maud Muller immortalized the setting hen in much the same way Riley immortalized the frost on the pumpkin. As a kid, there was no more depressing and agonizing thing for a youngster to hear when he went about the nightly chore stint than to be reminded: "Now don't forget to lift off the settin' hens."

Back in those pre-incubator days, there was never anything more tenaciously stubborn than a clucking, brooding, settin' hen intent on motherhood. She was truly devoted to duty, and would seldom budge from the nest atop a covey of 12-14 eggs unless she was lifted off. The call of "Chickie! Chickee! Chickee!" intoned by the feeder of the flock never ruffled a feather on her. She'd rather go without her cracked corn and wheat than to budge from her condominium of sweet smelling hay. She'd sit there on her nest like a tenant being evicted by the sheriff. Mother said those settin' hens just had to be fed. Always.

Lift 'em off, indeed! It was easy enough for her to say —she knew just exactly how to follow through on the removal of the setting hen. She'd gently approach her from the front, and very gently slip her two hands under the hen's wishbone—and with a "Nice chickee! Nice chickee!" tone in her patient voice very tenderly lift her off the nest. Nothing to it, when you did it right.

Her system never worked with us kids. That dedicated chick-a-biddy would peck us from the wrists to the elbows. So, we used our own method of getting her off the nesting homestead. We knew only one successful way of getting them to be companionable with the other chickens and "Eat up!" It was the quickest and most airborne way, catching them by the tail feathers in a crack-the-whip fashion. And it worked, too, while the tail feathers lasted. After that, every night till the three weeks of incubation were up, was measured in heart beats. . . Come to think of it, Mother used to own the biggest collection of bob-tailed hens to be seen anywhere.

It was always a gigantic task "breaking up" a setting

hen. It was always a battle of wits between the setting hen and Mother. The hen had promised herself she was going to have a home of her own and a family of her own, and Mother would have an adamant answer of "NO!" browned and ready on the fire. The cluck-a-biddy would cluck: "I'm goin' to do as I want to!" and Mother would come back with: "That's what you think!"

The usual preferred method of breaking up a clucking hen was to jail her for three days, and it always worked. The jail was a chicken coop especially built for having a mother hen and her chicks as occupants. It was a small A-shaped coop with bars across the front—the chickens could get out in the open and the mother stayed home clucking to them. One of those pogeys was used for the setting hen with big housekeeping ideas on her mind. After being locked up solo for three days, she forgot all about "A little gray home up North."

We kids always referred to the pogey-housed hen as being a "jailbird" and it was our task while she was jailed to see that she always had food and water taken to her, since she wasn't allowed trustee privileges. One of the kids once (Don't remember which one—H. B. doesn't remember doing it; Beulah wouldn't have done it, so it must have been one of the twins) took an elastic garter and wrapped it comfortably around the legs of the jailed clucker. The supposition was if she'd gotten herself jailed, she ought to be in handcuffs. Mother's only remark was: "I do declare. . . !" She often started that sentence and never, never finished it. Through the years, she never did get it completed.

## 12

# I'VE GOT MORE YESTERDAYS

WHATEVER HAPPENED TO ALL THE APPLES that were around when you and I were young, Maggie and John? What ever, ever did happen to them? There were the Russet apples most kids knew as "Rusti-Coats." They were a lovely olive brown color mottled with rusty patches through their skins. They were a rather small apple and were strictly for eating. They were a winter apple and recognized as "good keepers." And there were the Greenings, with their skins a rather nauseous green color, mixed with very tiny minute white spots speckling the green. Good for eating and par excellent for all cooking purposes. And a kid wrapping his hands around a huge Northern Spy apple, was like a football player wrapping his Atlas hands around a king-size hamburger. A kid would insert a pair of thumbs into the stem end of a Northern Spy apple, and it would open with a pop, a small explosion-like sound, that could be heard all the way from the dining room into the kitchen. Mother always knew how many Spy apples we kids were consuming, while doing our tomorrow's lessons seated around the long oak table in the dining room, by the number of pops she heard in the kitchen.

And there were the Ben Davis apples, definitely a winter apple that would keep in the roothouse till late May or June. They were a very hard apple that wouldn't have "cooked up" in three hours, and certainly weren't meant for old folks who preferred soft food. And what happened to Red Astrakan apples, also known to the kids as "Red Harvest" apples? They came along right after the 4th of July about the same time the Yellow Transparents made their appearance in the orchard. The Red Astrakans had a very distinctive taste, like the McIntosh apples we have today. It was a very individual taste, and you could tell blind-folded it was a Red Astrakan. The trees only bore fruit every other year—which, undoubtedly, is the reason why they aren't a-borning today in the abundant production lines of quick returns. Probably the exact reason why they dropped out of the running—they just couldn't cut the cider any more. And what happened to the favorite Maiden Blush apples? Just because not too many maidens blush any more really isn't any reason why the apples had to be expulsed from the orchards. And what happened to the Juicy Pippins, and the Grimes' Golden? They have been relegated into the limbo of Things That Were, and gone the way of the bird on Nellie's hat.

The answer given by horticulturists for the demise of yesteryear's favorite apple is that today's apple customers always insist on eye appeal first of all. Certainly, the Ben Davis apple would not have made center-fold in the *Apple Gap Magazine*—it just wasn't that handsome. Ben Davis who was to be "hung from a sour apple tree" (in the song) might have been sexy, but the apple by that name was strictly Dullsville. Very homely, so maybe this was the reason H. B. always had an affinity for them. "Pretty is as pretty does," you know. Please pass the applesauce—make it Northern Spy with cinnamon on top.

\*　　\*　　\*

Back when Mother was gardening, there was no going to a greenhouse or a seed store and getting tomato plants, half-grown and in blossom; and buying cabbage plants, and flowering annuals and hardy perennials already in full blossom. No, it was all done "from scratch" by planting the seeds and doing it the hard way. Mother always knew exactly what she wanted, had it all catalogued in her head. She had spent many hours in the little rocking chair poring over the seed catalogs when she wasn't patching, darning or knitting, deciding just exactly what she would be needing. There were many catalogs to choose from; they came through the winter months, and Mother must have been on the list of all the seed growers east of the Mississippi. A seed catalog arriving in the mail at Batten's Crossing could never be regarded as "junk mail." It was the most important mail that came, besides the first-class mail, of course.

We kids would look through the catalogs and put in our "two cents worth," and all at the same time. We always went for the varieties with beautiful names like "Dixie Belle" watermelons or "Stony Creek" watermelons, "Break o' Day" tomato seeds, "Pride of Shenandoah" string beans or "Pocahontas" pumpkin seeds. But year after year, Mother stuck to the old reliable names, the ones she knew from previous years would give and give. Always there'd be some fancy additions like cherry tomatoes and yellow ones for preserves. There'd be a little fancy lettuce, some endive, egg-plant or kohlrabi so the kids would get to know what it was.

When I was a very small child, probably six months old or less, Mother ordered seeds from the Department of Agriculture. All a farmer had to do was submit a requisition for the seeds they wanted to his Congressman, and that venerable gentleman carried the responsibility from there. Sometimes, that is. The proffered seeds "free for the asking" from the Government—a gift from Uncle Sam and Aunt Columbia, arrived in their little kraft envelopes. There were no psychedelic colored pictures on the package, just the plain how-to-do-it instructions. They were always excellent seeds, but one had to be sure and get the order in early to the Congressman. Mother said they probably carried the order around in their pockets for a month or so, whenever there was a delay. Sometimes the seeds wouldn't come till half-past dawg days, so Mother wasn't too crazy about Congressmen and seriously wondered if the one from our district could tell a hollyhock from a burdock.

. . . Wonder what would happen if I were to send a requisition order for seeds to my Congressman today. Shucks! He'd probably send a letter back saying: "My! What big ideas you have, Grandma!"

\*　　\*　　\*

None of us kids could remember the time when we were growing up when Dad was not deaf. Very, very deaf. He had been a riverboy on the Au Sable River in the days when timber was king in Michigan, and had ridden the foamy, frothy, churning water of the Au Sable down to the sawmills at Oscoda and Au Sable to Pack and Woods' Mill, Smith and Alger and Loud's Mill. It seems he had "come down" with a severe case of typhoid fever and had gone back to work too soon and developed a relapse, and the extreme case of deafness had resulted.

There were no hearing aids available then, but Dad developed the knack of lip-reading. If he were facing a person head-on and could see the physiognomy at all, he could read their lips with amazing accuracy, except the folks who wore a moustache—and that really messed up his talent. Just threw the lip-reading craft right out of business.

Dad, however, did wear a moustache himself. Always.

Except the time when all the kids coaxed him to shave it off—and then we didn't like it, and wanted it back on him again. Guess maybe we missed it most when we were washing dishes. All of the dishes outside the sugar bowl and creamer and a few odd pieces like the pepper and salt shakers that came as premiums in the big oatmeal boxes, were plain ironstone china. We missed that moustache cup every meal something awful. I cannot remember that any of us ever broke a moustache cup, so very carefully did we handle them while "doing dishes."

A couple different times in the middle of the night Mother heard a terrible ruckus in the chicken coop, and the next morning would find a chicken missing. No one ever saw her counting the chickens, but she always knew when one was missing. She set a trap one night, and next morning found a fat, sleek rat in the trap. She set the trap again, and a couple nights later heard the havoc again from the chicken coop. It was a terrible commotion made by the chickens, plus a dreadful awful squealing, night-rending sound.

The kids slept right through it and didn't hear a sound. Dad didn't hear anything, of course. Besides, who—who ever, ever read a chicken's lips?

But the melee from the chicken coop didn't miss Mother's acute ears. Mother headed for the chicken coop, clad in her night garments and some thin worn-out slippers on her feet, armed with a lantern and a new broom. We always had a new broom and an "old broom." The old broom had had its day and was worn down to the binding wires almost, and was used for sweeping off the floor of the long three-sided veranda that extended around the dining room and kitchen. And sometimes Mother used it—very, very seldom, to scrub the oak floors of the dining room and kitchen when she didn't get down on her hands and knees and use a scrubbing brush. She didn't use the broom very often, always felt like she was cheating when she did the cleaning that way.

She took the brand new broom and lantern, and headed

for the chicken coop ruckus. This time one quick look told her it wasn't a fat rat that had followed the Pied Piper and had gotten back. It wasn't that easy. The victim in the trap had an odorous smell that pervaded the summer night air, and it wasn't any morning dew coming down early. The animal squealing to high heaven, with a smell as far reaching, had a white stripe down the middle of his back and tail. He had both front feet caught in the trap and was fighting real crazy to get loose. Since the trap had been set outside the chicken coop door, right by the square hole for the chickens to make their entrances and exits, the chickens didn't get any of the impact of the animal's deadly weapon. But Mother got it, head-on!

Fearless, intrepid Mother, she released the squealing animal and went to the house and changed into a clean blue wrapper. It was in the early morning, and Mother built a small bonfire in the backyard and burned the night clothing and her old bedroom slippers, and the brand new broom. The lantern she took to the pump in the barnyard and scrubbed and scrubbed it with the old broom, using Gold Dust powder generously. Then she hung the lantern on a fence post by the pasture bars, for time and the elements to do their best with it. She returned to the back porch where the hired hands "washed up" before meals, where a basin of water and a clean roller towel were always waiting. She scrubbed and scrubbed and scrubbed, and was ready to call it a night.

No one had heard her, neither the kids nor the hired man, and Dad had slept right through it. Hadn't heard a sound, and certainly hadn't seen any lips moving in the dark. Mother had salvaged the lantern, but it had been a long day's work in the nighttime.

\* \* \*

One time Dad and I were sitting on the rail fence down the lane, and right in the middle of the summer a woodpecker was pecking and pecking on a rail. He'd wait a while and listen, wait and listen and then attack—acted like he hadn't eaten in a week. Sometimes when we sat on the fence we made up limericks, and now real quick-like Dad came up with one about the woodpecker. He told me that down in Kentucky and Georgia that woodpeckers were real thick, and that in Georgia they were called "Omigawd birds." It seemed that when strangers to Georgia saw the woodpeckers for the first time and watched their pecking maneuvers in the trees, they always said "Omigawd!" That winter when we went to the cedar swamp for the first time I pointed to a woodpecker poised on a tree trunk, ready for attack. I said to Dad: "Look quick, there's one of them Omigawd birds." He asked me where I'd heard that one, and I reminded him of its derivation. He said: "Let's forget what they call 'em down in Georgia—just forget you ever heard it." And I did forget it, too, 'til right now.

## 13

# YOU CAN TAKE
# THE GIRL
# OUT O' THE COUNTRY . . .

PROBABLY IN EVERY FAMILY THERE IS ALWAYS
one member who "burns with a short fuse," as the saying
goes. In our family, Pearl would have won the unquestion-
able honor hands down. Like the Chinese, she too, used
acupuncture—only hers was a different process, she used
verbal acupuncture.

A definite "spitfire," she could slay anyone with twenty-
five easy words or less. Dad said once she would have made
a great Attorney General.

After Ida was married, Pearl was the oldest one left at
home. And at that domicile there was always work to be
done, four seasons of it. No indeed, four seasons around our
place didn't mean the name of a posh restaurant, and it
didn't have anything to do with the weather—it meant the
duration of the work pattern. It was just never, never done:
kids to be fed, kids to be cleaned up, their lunches to be
packed and gotten off to school. Pearl often did housework

for new mothers in the neighborhood. No 40-hour week, those hired-girl "working out" sessions. She soon discovered that the kids at the new place were hungrier than the ones she knew at home. And the new babies, not one of them ever came "potty trained." The only difference about the faces she scrubbed and got off to school, the new faces had different angles, different grimaces, different pout lines than the ones she knew at home. The stipend stopped at three dollars a week, and sometimes less.

Pearl thought of liberation years and years before it was ever mentioned in the newspapers. Like brother George, she too, got infected with the wanderlust, and wanted "out." She had long had the feeling she wanted to be a nurse. And it is probably a blessing for the medical profession she never followed through and became a Florence Nightingale. As a surgical nurse, she probably would have operated on the doctor. A disagreeable patient probably would have been wearing a chapeau in the form of a bedpan tucked firmly below the ears.

Pearl finally "flew the nest" and she landed in Ann Arbor, Michigan. Her first employment was in a professor's family where the head of the household was an instructor at the University of Michigan. There were three boys in the family, and they loved her secretly and madly. Undoubtedly, it was the wonderful food she prepared for them. Always cookies were on hand; sour cream cookies, soft molasses gingerbread men with candy buttons down their fronts, and fat scalloped sugar cookies with a huge raisin in the middle of each of them. They were wild, unbridled little hellions who couldn't be bothered with the little nuisances of "Thank you!" and "Please!"

She enrolled in night school and took a commercial course. Not just typing and shorthand, but bookkeeping to make doubly sure she'd click in one department. She was a whiz at shorthand, and the bookkeeping instructor immediately labeled her "Univac." And that was before the word was invented!

## You Can Take the Girl Out o' the Country

Her new employers recognized and appreciated her worth, and often told her so. They gave her frequent small bonuses, and secured tickets for her to attend operas, concerts, lectures and shows. She attended operas and, of course, didn't understand what they were about. But it was a genuine and altruistic treat to be in the huge Hill Auditorium and exposed to how "the other half lived." The nonchalant other half, the folks who hadn't been raised by narrow-gauge railroad tracks, and probably had never known the nostril-repelling smell of a springtime field with a deluge of freshly-spread manure offending the sunshine, and offending more and more as the sunshine got sunnier and sunnier. She browsed through mammoth book stores and prestigious art stores. 'Twas like going to Heaven but, somehow, you just never, never, thought you'd be going quite so soon.

Meanwhile back on the farm, Amy had married the hired man who was currently working for Dad. He was from Nebraska and crazy about horses which, of course, made him an okay-guy in Dad's book. He always "grained" the horses at noon before he came in the house to eat his own meal. That gesture alone made a big hit with Dad. He curried and curried them, and always "rested" them out in the fields, the same way Dad had always babied them. Dan and Amy's 80-acre farm was right in back of the Home Place just beyond the creek flats.

Years later when equine talent had relegated into obsolescence on the farm and Dan had bought his first tractor, he always said all the fun had gone out of farming. It sure wasn't any fun to walk up to a tractor and hit it with a resounding slap on the rotunda and say: "Let's go! There's harrowing to be done, ole girl!" He always missed the horses most in wintertime—said a barn just wasn't the same without the good old horsey smell dominating the whole barn. Even the barn swallows didn't seem to be too crazy about a barn that didn't have horses for tenants. "Who ever heard a tractor whinny?" he used to say in disgust.

Amy, the patient one, and endowed with the sweetest disposition of any of the seven girls, was married. Endowed also with Mother's green thumbs, she always had a bountiful garden. She grew things like Brussel sprouts, endive, oak leaf lettuce and fancy tomatoes. One year the white-tailed deer jumped over the woven wire fence by an adjoining woods and picnicked in her garden overnight. They ate cabbage, kohlrabi, Brussel sprouts, letuce, turnips, beets— went down the rows and accomplished a cleanup job on everything. Amy was bewildered, but said maybe the deer were lacking in Vitamin C and went hunting for it. Next year she planted an enormous garden, figured half of it for the deer and the other half for themselves. But it didn't turn out that way. That summer she had twice as many deer.

Beulah had finished Normal School and taught in an elementary school for a year. Beulah, the perennial student herself, the eternal bookworm—always in quest of more and more knowledge, knew school-teaching was not for her. One year was enough. Very sufficient. Positively too much; she knew positively she wasn't "teacher material." Her next job was at the money order window at the Jackson, Michigan postoffice where she worked for many years. Each summer her vacations took her in different directions, one year to Manitoba, Canada, to visit relatives and to see the Canadian wheatfields she had read so much about, fields so large they consumed a whole section of land; another vacation was spent in the New England states; there was a junket to Texas to see if it was as great as the Texans said it was, and to see the cattle; a trip to New Mexico and Arizona to see the cactus plants and the desert vastness. She went to Florida, to California, to Hawaii . . . always in quest of enlightenment. Like Uncle DeLormey, she never liked Michigan winters, and decided very suddenly to move to California. This was back before the outdoor ceiling was laden with smog, and on a clear sunny day one could see Catalina Island from Los Angeles.

Tractors can't have babies—
and they don't give the barn that nice horsey smell.

## Blow for Batten's Crossing!

Beulah had always maintained she wasn't going to be in a hurry to get married, insisted that when, and IF she did, the guy would have to be much more intelligent than she was. Summary: she married an author, a playwright no less. The walls of their home were carpeted with books; the floors were piled with books—piled like cordwood back on the farm. Maverick Terrell, her husband, had been a son of two famous cattle families in Texas, the Mavericks and the Terrells. "Mav" was a prolific writer, an enchanting conversationalist and a masterful after-dinner speaker. Always words and more words at his disposal, both prose and poetry. He translated French poetry into English, and vice versa. Yes, Beulah the perennial student, the former "teacher's pet," had married an encyclopedia of universal knowledge.

After twenty-some years of marriage and living in Ann Arbor, Pearl's husband suddenly passed away, and after a short time Pearl went to California to live. She took a refresher course in accounting, and joined the employed. Pearl, the diligent worker and spitfire extraordinary, was working in a large hospital on the night shift from 11 p.m. to 7 a.m. All alone working on "spooky bills" in readiness for patients' discharges in the morning. She hated the stilly still in the hospital office as badly as she had disliked some of the stilly after-dark nights back on the farm.

Back home always there was the mournful dirge of the tree toads, the katydids not settled down for the night, and the annoying branches of the crabtree outside the bedroom window scratching against the house on windy nights. There was the nightly barking of dogs in the distance, and the answering back by our old dog, Prince. At the hospital, the stilly nights were interpolated with tinkling of bells of someone being paged. Allegedly, the walls were soundproof, but her Maud Muller ears picked up every sound and heard all messages.

After a couple hectic, frenzied weeks, she blew—she blew right out the door! Real quick-like, like right now!

The same tenacity that had made her a spitfire and a short-burning fuse also made her an exacting accountant. Next job was in an elegant dress shop frequented by ultra-best actresses in Hollywood. The jet set before jet. There must have been a peephole or lookout arrangement in the upstairs offices because the office workers could look down on the main floor as the curvaceous beauties of the flickers came in to execute their lavish and extravagant shopping.

The one thing that seemed to perturb the working girls was a trait many of the actresses had. They'd remove their luxurious coats, jackets or stoles by letting them slip off their shoulders to the floor, and stand on them while they leisurely shopped for hose, lingerie, and such. Pearl preferred Marjorie Main to any of them. There was no putting-on shenanigans with her; and to someone like Pearl who had worn black sateen bloomers and scratchy, jaggedy hand-knit woolen stockings as a youngster, Marjorie was always exactly as she appeared on the screen—just plain Maw Kettle. Shucks! And great ringing bell of Ole Cherry! She was just like the folks from back Alcona County way. More specifically, she was like the folks from Batten's Crossing.

# 14

# THE SISTERS AND THEIR MISTERS

THE TWINS, JUNE AND JEAN—THE PRETTY ONES
with the black laughing eyes and the black, black hair,
both received a good musical education. Jean, an accomplished accordionist, traveled for seven years with USO
shows. She knew the pleasure of entertaining the boys in
camp, and remembered the courage it sometimes sapped
from her when she took her accordion into Veteran's hos-
pitals. Jean—the prompt ad-libber, the voracious kidder—
was always a treat to the incapacitated, lonesome GIs. Several years after returning from the USO tours, she married
an orthopedic doctor in California.

I remember it well: that girl was a picture that's for
sure, astride Champ or Jess while cultivating corn back on
the farm. For some reason, Dad always had one of the
kids ride on the horse's back when he cultivated corn, probably because from that vantage point a rider could negotiate
a sharper turn at the end of the row than he could do behind

the cultivator, and thus not tramp down as much corn in the process of cultivating right up close to the fence row. Corn tramped down with the horse's feet always required first-aid treatment with the hoe, and much elbow grease.

There was Jean, ten or twelve years old, astride the heavy farm horse delighted with her perch on a summer's day. Champ and Jess at one time had been a matched pair of dappled grays (Prettiest horses in the county Dad always said), but a few years had turned their bodies to a pale silver gray-white while the hips remained the original beautiful dappled gray. There would be black-haired Jean in her bright calico dress—with her long black pigtails with red ribbon bows at the end of the pigtails, her nutmeg-brown childish gams dangling over each side of the horse's strong white shoulders. Blue, blue skies overhead, and large cumulus clouds hanging down from upstairs . . . summer coming down, corn growing overnight and going to be knee-high by the Fourth of July . . . going to be as high as an elephant's eye some day, you betcha! Jean made a pretty sight, a very pretty farm picture. Today, she drives the L. A. Freeway each day, driving with the assurance of Mario Andretti going around in circles at Indianapolis on May 30th. Little girl, you have grown!

June married an "efficiency expert" who flew back and forth across the country advising large businesses the way to run their establishments in an efficient manner. June who had always loved beautiful clothes and beautiful things—and who probably was on excellent terms with charge accounts, learned the correct, judicious and "efficient" way to handle money. She learned how to budget her time, how to budget money, and even learned a few tricks of her own on how to outsmart the budget. After she was widowed for several years following the sudden death of her husband, she married a violinist with the Chicago Symphony Orchestra, Arnold Price, known to fellow members as "Priceless." The large orchestras of the country were coming upon leaner times, and he transferred from the

Photo by H. Girard

High as an elephant's eye—and growing.

symphonic world to the commercial, and became a veep with a large wholesale jewelry firm.

Widowed again, she currently lives in a high-rise apartment looking out on Lake Michigan: blue skies, seagulls and ships, and Chicago from her 22nd floor retreat. She has retained her abundant humility, and remembers fondly raking hay, pitchin' hay, picking potato bugs, and lifting setting hens off the nest. Like Mother, adept at needlework, she does creative knitting, designs her own needlepoint projects, and makes venturesome hooked rugs. A hooked rug on her kitchen floor has a white cat in it named Phoebe, probably reminds her of the cats back on the farm.

Back there we had a calico cat named Fanny. It was a yellow, white, gray, fawn, rusty-brown and black cat—looked like a patchwork quilt, only it was made of cat. Fanny was the only cat Mother allowed in the house—she stayed behind the Kalamazoo wood range and purred at the smells emanating from the oven, and you never would have known she was around. Once we kids had a kitten we called Spearmint because his tail was wriggley. Dad asked one time if we hadn't reached a little on that one. June's cat on her kitchen rug looks like one of our barnyard cats that hung around at milking time waiting for a big dish of warm milk fresh out of the tap.

Memories of grown-up June and Jean hark back to the time when Mother dressed them up every day to sit and watch on the "banks" of land on each side of the narrow-gauge tracks. They'd wait for the coming of the little A.S.&N.W. train. The engineer would "Toot! Toot!" and they'd wave back and laugh hilariously and he'd Toot! Toot! five or six times real close together, and it sounded like a train laughing. That ritual went on for years during their early childhood. Today, dern it! they still get whistled at.

Hazel, the homely one, never, of course, made Miss America. Not even Miss Alcona County . . . Shucks! she couldn't even have made Miss Batten's Crossing. She married a schoolteacher, a very serious-minded school-teacher. A captain is sometimes said to run a tight ship. He ran a quiet schoolhouse. All serenity, no monkey business, a dedicated devotion to teaching that the kids remembered to adulthood. He always said he never had a youngster who couldn't learn.

He had been raised in an orphanage after his mother had died in childbirth. At the age of eight, he was placed in a foster home of a devout Methodist couple who didn't believe in too much merriment. Positively, no frivolities. At the orphanage, it seems, the kids called him "Romey" when they weren't chanting "Joseph Jerome Girard! . . . Joseph Jerome Girard!" in sing-song fashion, so the foster parents called him Jay. His friends called him J. J.

As a kid on a rocky, hilly, unproductive farm in Ohio, he walked three miles to school, and three miles home again. Life became earnest, filled with a serious intent to get a good education, and off the farm. It was in the section of Ohio close to the Malabar Farm made famous by Louis Bromfield—who converted a rock-strewn, impover-ished farm to fertile fields of agricultural wonderment by "plowing under" for years legumes and all precious organic matter.

J. J.'s family moved to northern Michigan to escape the ravishing rigors of hay fever each long summer. It was there he met the girl from Batten's Crossing—Yeah, you guessed it, the homely one with hundreds and hundreds of freckles, and a pug nose that still headed straight upstairs like it was smelling something bad in the attic. Long, lanky —six feet tall, almost, and who wore clothes like they were still on the hanger.

For a couple years Mother tried to do something about the bosom situation. But it seemed what Mother Nature didn't endow, our Mother Batten just couldn't change, no how. She fashioned creations of yards and yards of nar-row embroidered edging sewed to sturdy double thicknesses of muslin. This was fastened to camisole straps with dainty gold safety pins. It didn't have any more chance of leaving the depot than a pair of red suspenders would have in leaving the premises. She put a lot of time, a lot of love, into those creations but her best efforts would never have put the modern day counterpart of Warner's or Maidenform out of business.

The first flattering bra H. B. ever owned was bought from a door-to-door representative of the Real Silk Hosiery Company. They manufactured silk hosiery of high repute that wore and wore, and for which the slaving silkworms probably never received any fringe benefits. The saleslady with a ready tape measure and a miraculous delicate touch measured the unpretentious bosom and said it would have to be a 32AA. She Tut! Tutted! through her teeth and said it really should be 30 inches, but they just weren't made that small, and suggested it wouldn't take but a minute to "run up" a half-inch tuck on each side. "No big trick!" she analyzed.

H. B. out-twigged Twiggy by dozens of years. And it got her exactly nowhere with plenty of acceleration. "As the twig is bent, so grows the tree," said the old adage. The tree must have been a Joshua tree—it never did have good architecture.

J. J.'s folks didn't think too much of H. B. becoming a member of the family. "All the Battens are 'educated fools' and Hazel's the biggest one of the lot," was the ready appraisal when they were told by him he had made a selection. They liked the literary "stuff" she did for David C. Cook Publishing Company: nature articles, brief Biblical profiles, inspirational essays that appeared in Sunday School publications, but right there the admiration for her printed endeavors stopped icy cold. They disliked with an intensity the carefree, nonchalant material authored by her in newspapers and farm magazines. Anyone who wrote in that crazy style would have to be one awful sloppy housekeeper. Just bound to be . . . just couldn't miss! He should marry a schoolteacher, and they'd have something in common.

Marv Girard at age 13—the thinker,
the poet, the artist, and teacher's distress.

There were always children, too, to be thought about, and with two schoolteachers as parents the kids were bound to be smart.

Did J. J. and H. B. ever have smart kids! Two of them, one double smart and the other extra smart. There was Vic, the hardy perennial "teacher's pet" who galloped through the first, second and third grades in one year. And there was Marv, three years younger, the perennial "teacher's torment." At the age of five, Vic showed a definite proclivity for mathematics, and today does the disgusting thing of doing conglomerate multiplication "in his head" and percentage from the same derivation before anyone else can draw a pencil. Marv started kibitzing at the age of five, and through all his school years fast-talked himself out of perplexing situations. Always talented in art, he successfully garnered a "D--(D double minus) in art in his senior year of high school. One day, it seems, he protested drawing again a giant Hubbard squash that had been brought into class for the art lesson. Marv jumped to his feet, in verbal rebellion, and requested an answer: "Why, WHY must we always be drawing deep wrinkles in a stupid squash? Why, WHY can't we just once dig down into our knobby pointed heads (he pointed to his own pyramid) and draw something with action to it—like it had muscles, like it was alive . . . a horse, a bull, a rooster on a fence. Anything, anything at all, kind benevolent Heaven, but another squash split open and its bowels showing and wrapped in wrinkles deep as furrows. Why, teacher, WHY?"

When the class annual, *The Spic* came out that year at graduation time, no mention was made that he had been a member of the art club, or that he had contributed many sketches and cartoons to the *Spic,* or that he had been a band member for four years. His handsome physiognomy was there on the page all by itself, without any printed adornment around it whatsoever. He looked bare as a radish.

In Government class, he was the students' hero. Every day he shot to his feet—and extolled his ideas, and he had many, but they didn't happen to coincide with the teacher's. One of the World wars was on—it couldn't have been the First one, and 18-year-olds were being lassoed the minute they graduated from high school that year, and Marv wasn't particularly enthralled about the mission or time involved. He jumped to his feet, pulled out his wallet which probably didn't have more than one picture of George Washington in it, and certainly none of Abraham Lincoln, Alexander Hamilton and Andrew Jackson ensconced on a green background, and proclaimed: "This is the cause of war. . . ," etcetera, etcetera. The kids loved it (it was taking up time and making the hours pass quicker). He looked like a youthful William Jennings Bryan giving with his "Cross of Gold" oration—all the while brandishing his five-dollar Christmas billfold with a lonely buck in it. The teacher said: "Girard, go to the principal's office!"

The principal had seen that physiognomy before, many times before—he'd have missed it painfully if he hadn't seen it two or three times a week. He told J. J., it seems, that most of the time he found himself agreeing with the glib-talking, volcanic-minded youth. Said he had even gotten to the place where he told him to sit down and linger while in the office, like he was really getting the "One-two!" in the principal's office, and would finally say to him: "Girard, you better go back to class now."

That guy, Marv, never did learn how to draw a squash. But he has known the victorious pleasure of receiving checks for gag cartoons—both in U.S. and Canada, and good ole Oscar Mezulla for sketches in Western magazines. He'll draw curvaceous girls, fat women bulging with mirth, bow-legged waddies, whiskered lumberjacks, fractious horses rearin' back on two hind legs like Ole Nell, and bulls with their heads down, pawing the ground like Jasper, our Jersey bull back on the farm—but the wrinkled squash he leaves for the seed catalogs to glorify.

## KEEPER OF THE PINES

When I was young I heard the wind
Laughing down aisles of tall timber.
The wind laughed me a melody
From out of the wilderness . . . I made
It my cradle song.

When I was young I heard Chippewas
Making wigwam talk at sundown.
Bronze faces spoke to each other
About perch and corn . . . and
Tomorrow. I've got birch bark
Talk for a memory . . . I've got
Buckskin words for a Yesterday.

When I was young I heard wild geese
Honking pathways through autumn.
Restless wings traced their farewells
On a frosted sky.
I promised them springtime
To come back to . . . and Home.

When I was young I heard the moonless
Starless cry of the wolf pack.
Gray hunters killed on nights
Of the new snow . . . And I understood.
I was one of them.

When I was young I heard lumberjack
Echoes across high rollways of winter.
Big shoulders laughed . . . and worked
And swore. I gave them a river
And a monument to remember me by.

I am keeper of the pines.
I am the Great Outdoors.
I am God's country.
I am Michigan.

      *—Marvin Eugene Girard*

# 15

# HERE'S GLENNIE—OOPS!
# YOU MISSED IT

J. J. DECIDED THE MONETARY REWARDS OF school-teaching, which for years and years had been pegged at 100-115 dollars a month, were woefully inadequate for raising a family, and could see no forseeable increase in what he knew would always be his favorite occupation. He changed employment and became the village postmaster. Postmaster of Glennie, Michigan, with a population notated in the census "Good Book" as 100 inhabitants. The postmastership of a fourth-class post office includes the privilege of having a place of business to supplement the base pay from Uncle Sam and Aunt Columbia, plus a percentage of the postage cancellation, governs the payment of the job—or did at that time.

Glennie was "up the pike" from Lott, Michigan, which was "up the way" a mile from Batten's Crossing. For years and years, and more years, there had been nothing at Batten's Crossing but kids and more kids. Kids hanging from the trees, kids atop the horses, kids picking potato bugs, kids playing "Ante-ante-I-over" the woodshed roof. There was the farm, of course, with the barns and fields on one side of the narrow-gauge tracks, and the house, the windmill, and the beautiful gardens on the other side. For many years, the house had been painted a pea green color—Sears, Roebuck's best, believe it was called Seroco. It was an excellent paint, and had the endurance of the Sphinx. Never blistered, never faded, never chalked, never peeled—just endured winter's blizzards and summer's scorching.

Lott, Michigan, where all the Batten kids attended school had a post office, a wee grocery store in the same building, a one-room schoolhouse and a church.

Glennie, Michigan, is still on the Michigan maps—up Alcona County way. Look, my hearties, and you will find it. Nearly everyone's been there, has heard about it, knows someone there, or plans on going there sometime. Batten's Crossing and Lott are no longer on the map, like Maiden Blush apples and the Audubon feathers on Nellie's hat, they have disappeared into the Things That Were, disappeared with the termination of the A.S.&N.W. railroad. The narrow-gauge tracks were removed, and the right-of-way reverted back to the original owners. Only the village church at Lott remains in that little town, proud and pearly-white, with its bell pealing from its high belfry. The church, built in 1905, has been preserved as nearly as possible in its original form. The tiny maple floor boards are sanded satin-smooth; the high ceilings remain as they were; the statistics of last week's attendance at church and Sunday School indicate a good representation; the church bell is an inviting sound on Sunday mornings when church bells are heard but very infrequently these days.

Yes, J. J. was a village postmaster. Instead of being in a schoolhouse and looking at two youthful fingers extended in frantic "V" formation, meaning: "Please, teacher, may I leave the room?", he was hearing the wistful intonation:

"I MUST surely have some mail today." For several years, each summer the town was visited by the Community Chautauqua, bringing the best in diversified talent a nation had to offer. No "X-rating, no R-rating" sequences at any time; it was earthy entertainment that even the twelve disciples would have enjoyed. The first time this chronicler ever heard the question asked: "Does the Spearmint lose its Flavor on the Bedpost Overnight?" it was queried by the renowned Willie Howard. Some of the farmers almost lost their galluses laughing over that one. They had left their harvest fields waiting—for miles and miles around, to "come to Chautauqua," and were loving every minute of it. And, year after year, the emcee told the proud citizens of Glennie that they were "the smallest town in the United States big enough to support a Chautauqua" and their galluses always fit more snugly after that accolade.

The exodus of tourists to northern Michigan had just begun with enthusiasm, so an ice cream parlor, candy store, and miscellaneous items such as souvenirs of the north country were the auxiliary items offered for sale besides postage stamps. (Postage stamps and soda-jerking are both sticky jobs with slow profits.) J. J. connived the idea of having a commercial photographer take pictures of the surrounding scenic spots and lakes to be made into postcards for the tourist trade. H. B.'s pug nose tilted further upstairs when she looked at the finished photographic postcards. "I could do better'n that with a Brownie camera on my pointed head," she made the disgusted appraisal. "Look at those pictures of beautiful Vaughan Lake," she groaned. "William Brady back in the Civil War days could have done better'n that," she continued to anguish. She and her dad had decided a long time ago, sitting on a rail fence, what would really make a good picture. They were armchair photographers on a wormy, woodpecker-pecked rail fence, doing an Edward Weston arrangement of every beautiful landscape in sight. "An Indian wouldn't be caught in the Happy Hunting Ground taking a picture of birch trees and making such a clutter of it. Just a few of them at the water's edge are all that is needed . . . one doesn't need a hundred of them piled up like rocks on a rockpile . . . That guy's imagination has to be all in his taste buds," she nagged.

Probably, it was that photographer's interpretation of beautiful scenic material that directed H. B.'s attention to photography in the following years. She wanted simple pictures that told a story with impact, clean-cut composition without clutter. Just one main point of view, not a half dozen or more things vieing for "head of the class" attention.

. . . There was the clergyman who was once asked to write a brief paragraph on the Grand Canyon. He wrote something like this: "Yesterday I stood on the rim of the Grand Canyon and viewed God's greatest handiwork." A Boy Scout was asked to jot down his impression. He scribbled this masterpiece: "Yesterday I stood on the rim of the Grand Canyon and spit a mile."

What is seen in a landscape or seascape always depends on the eyes of the beholder. The early tourists to northern Michigan must have liked what they saw. At first, tourists "to the sticks" were a scarce commodity—folks from Ohio, Indiana and Illinois mostly, who came north to beat the hay fever they had experienced during dawg days of the year before. The first tourists to the coot-and-hern country often had to chase cattle off the road before they could continue on their way. Cows were still feeding "out on the commons." Chickens were crossing the road, sir, for the same reasons they have always had for crossing the road—to get on the other side. Irritated geese were yelling "What! What! What!" at the top of their alarm systems. Nervous guinea hens were atop rail fences and screaming in a steady cadence of "Buckwheat! Buckwheat! Buckwheat!"

The home folks were rather skeptical about tourists at first. They were looked upon as white-collared gallivanters—gross and net, who didn't have another thing to do

but drive their "spiffy cars" through Apple Gap and Onion-
ville at a speed . . . well, some of the natives said it was
"like hell bent for election!" And some elections do end
up there, I've heard.

They had ravenous appetites for city slickers—ate like
incinerators, and weren't too particular about the fare,
just so there was plenty of it. It surely took a heap of butter,
eggs, milk and fresh vegetables to keep them sustained.
They made an awful fuss over scenic effects, just like Michigan was an open-space Sharon. They'd lean against a
sapling and let compassionate gloaming close in around
them. First-class laughing folks they were, all of them,
life-loving, ravenous, and happy-happy. Not one of them
suggested a high-hat, a big false alarm or a know-it-all.
They were folksy folks liking what they saw. They'd soak
their burny bunions and their corny corns in the Au Sable
River and think they had new feet—the same Au Sable
River that in its springtime heyday had floated centennial
pines down its white waters to found a nation. They looked
at the plutocratic maples in their dress suits and come-to-
Heaven collars, at the oaks, birches and elms everywhere
that were here long before J. Sterling Morton gave Arbor
Day to the world. Most of all, those tourists loved the pine
trees—pines much older than they were themselves, pines
that had seen the passing of the Indians, the Jesuit fathers,
of hunters, traders and trappers—living historical records
of the Great Alchemist's power "to make a tree!"

And then something happened. Folks sat up and
started to take notice. Why! it was really the tourists, and
not they, who really appreciated the homeland's attributes.
Seemed as if they had been too busy with crops, this, that
and the other things, that they just hadn't looked around
much, or maybe had gotten used to the prodigal natural
resources about them and took it all pretty much for
granted. Right then and there, farmers quit calling tourists
"tin canners" and settled down to the business of flouting
their best hospitality, and giving the enthusiastic new-

comers a rousing glad-hand, a wish-you-well handshake that "took" like a Methodist handshake after the church services.

Localities within the tourist scope, and that included any place with a lake and good fishing, found themselves profiting from the influx of tourists. Probably the early tourists did much to bring picnics into their present popularity. Why! those folks would sit out under a canopy of sunlight, eat plain bread 'nd butter sandwiches with a lettuce leaf intact, and think they were at a banquet. Meanwhile they'd drink the climate, eat it, and fill their pockets with enough oxygen, pure and unspoiled, to last a couple weeks.

People began to realize that they didn't have to spend an embryo fortune to enjoy themselves on vacation. Some gas and oil in the old jalopy, a few green bills and some small change and a road map were the chief requisites. Then came life, and the pleasant campfires: coffee, dozens of fish, bread 'nd butter, and quiet rest in the burning noontide. Pretty soon things started to happen—everyone came down with a picnic complex or got a compound fracture of the wanderlust. So, every summer's day now is picnic day in Michigan. Some people, severely addicted, will even picnic in the rain. Some rabid picnickers picnic in winter. And love it.

Somehow, taking the edible ABCs out in the open was a great way to kindle an appetite or pacify the old one. Thinking came clear, and the mind didn't run a network of rabbit paths that twist and turn and double back on themselves. Overhead the blue sky flung like the bow of promise. They wanted to sit right down and write the gardener, Maw Nature. Someone has said that all the eats at a picnic began with the letter "B"—buns, beans, burgers, bologna and bugs. The last one probably has reference to the bugs that are so indigenous to potato salad or the ants, maybe, that pantomime the Charge of the Light Brigade the minute that apple pie shows its crust on the scene.

Gardens were made larger to supply the voracious ones; cottages were built by forest-rimmed lakes; free tourists camps were opened, and hospitality took on a new girth line. And now, even the most ardent of the erstwhile prejudiced ones are willing to admit that the tourist crop is one of Michigan's best. Plant good seeds, and the harvests are bound to be better. Just plain good farming principles— the same theories that Uncle Hi had always set to the sweet music of his success, and his cash register.

On one occasion I asked a scholarly-looking chap, with perfumed vowels and disinfected consonants, just what one feature he had enjoyed most of a canoe trip from Grayling to Oscoda (from the head of the Au Sable River to the foot of it). After much stroking of his academical beard, he thought it was a bend in the river where he had taken off his shoes and sox, and walked on a mossy log over and over again. It had taken 25 years off his shoulders, he knew.

A good log-walker myself, ever since the days of crossing the mossy log in the creek flats of the Home Place to get on the other side, his venture didn't sound too exciting to me at first. Until I heard his story. In a well-groomed voice that always seemed to wear an ascot and top hat, he went on and on . . . telling about those other days, boyhood days he had almost forgotten, when his ragged pantaloons always had a fishy smell from conveying fish home in his pockets; hilarious hours when he had pitted his speed and strength against the flight of grasshoppers and sold 'em for ten cents a dozen, for bait. Bloated, white-bellied bullfrogs lollying on lily pads, dragon flies flashing in the sunlight . . . He had known and loved it all, and had forgotten them till a bend in the river dared to challenge his memory.

Twenty years, think of it! That's a long time to keep hoeing and not see the end of the row; it's a long time to go without a song in your heart. Twenty years of pulsating life slipping by, and you holding a pedagogical headache;

141

twenty years of keeping primped and feathers preened, and
never feeling a mossy log under your bare feet, and never
daring a reckless gesture like playing a harmonica solo on
a freshly-buttered ear of Golden Bantam corn.

"How come . . . How come?" I asked him. "How come
you don't just dig yourself a nice comfortable hole, like a
grave, maybe, and zipper it shut after you, how come?"

He said he'd go back to the mossy log and think about
it a few hours first. The next time he came to the stamp
window, a couple weeks later, I scarcely recognized him.
His shirt was open at the neck to give his Adam's apple free-
wheeling; his ears were sunburned till they stood out like
miniature red sails in the sunset. He'd been fishing, hiking,
boating and blistering. The academical whiskers were gone
(said he'd used 'em for fish bait). His face was as bare as
Whittier's little man with cheeks of tan, with turned-up
pantaloons and merry-whistled tunes.

His two weeks' vacation stretched to all summer. And
what a change. Gone were the ten-gallon words with which
he had staggered the natives, and his shirt tail was usually
out like an awning. His hat was populated with trout flies
that had been sold to him, said all he had to do now was
to sell the flies to the fish. He could puncture the very mild
expression of "Dern it, now!" with more enthusiasm than
any of the talented suspender-snappers of the local Spit
and Whittle club. And all because a bend in the river where
turtles slipped off mossy logs into the liquid depths, and
kingfishers honked upstream, had dared to turn back the
kilocycles of time, and because he had the courage to be
himself.

A blush-faced fireman from the hook-and-ladder crew
of an Akron, Ohio, fire squad once told me, without
apology, there wasn't anything he enjoyed quite so much
on a vacation after a lucky day of fishing than to sit lazily
by a campfire at night and watch the dying embers. Just to
know there had been a whopping, jolly good fire, without
any damage, and he hadn't had to budge from his tracks,

was the height of restful ecstacy to him. Next best, he enjoyed listening to the clanging of cowbells as the cows waited patiently at the pasture bars to be milked. Let 'em jangle their sirens, dern it! he wasn't their keeper, their milk plumber, and it was sweet music to ears that had become jaded from too many fire gongs. So ring out, Cherry and Pinkie, Dinah and Brindle, Abigal and Tess. Ring out, kind therapeutic bells! Maybe a frenzied, frazzled fireman is resting.

You never can tell what might possibly spell vacation for the other person . . . like the preacher and the spitting Boy Scout, looking at the Grand Canyon, they both found something different. Michigan with her wide diversity of outdoor appeals lends herself well to an open-space Sharon of Vacationland. Her rain-washed and wind-blown scenery salutes all onlookers with the same salutation: "Top of the morning, folks!" or "The benisons of eventide to you-all!"

## 16

# COME BACK AGAIN, ARCHIBALD

AFTER A PROLONGED ILLNESS, THE DOCTORS insisted much rest was required by H. B. with much time to be spent outdoors in the sunlight and fresh air, so the Girards were on the move again. They moved to Tawas City, with beautiful Tawas Bay out the back door.

Tawas Bay at that time had not yet become crowded with cabins and cottages around its perimeter. One could walk and walk along the beach, and encounter only the fish houses and the occasional small boats tied up at the shoreline. Tawas City had the nearest skies I ever saw. They were like a big floppy blue hat with white blossoms on it. They were skies that dipped way down to the rim of the bay—and when you stood off at a distance, it seemed the seagulls on the shore were walking into the clouds.

Gulls have always been a very fascinating study to me— we didn't have them in the briar patches back home. The

Tawas Bay, Michigan, provided many driftwood goodies
after a bad storm.
Teen-age beachcomer adds to his collection.

take-off of a wild duck is a pretty sight; the soaring hawk is a memorable picture, but for rare combination of swift grace and useful precision there is nothing to equal the play of gulls above the surface of water.

I have watched stalwart lumberjacks cement new peas into a base of mashed potatoes and convey the finished concoction to its destination with a dexterity that would have done justice to a Le Tourneau earth-mover. I have seen brawny hay-makers, with ruddy cheeks and prominent Adam's apples, stow away giant wedges of blueberry pie with a gusto and velocity that would make a pelican seem "mincey" by comparison. And I've seen expert fishermen, whipping a stream, display a finesse that was fascinating. But none of them, however graceful, can lay claim to the beauty and agility with which the gull takes his calories from ocean, lake or river.

Those gulls that strolled the beach at Tawas Bay would eat anything. Anything. Anytime. Apples, hot dogs, smoked herring, Michigan dill pickles, Jewish dill pickles, Polish dill pickles, garlic dill pickles. Name it, they'd eat it. They'd eat it even if it didn't have a name. Popcorn, puffed wheat, crackerjacks, salted peanuts, Mary-Janes and Jujy-fruits. Toast with peanut butter was a big thing with them. The kids had two favorite gulls—one was called Gulligan Gull and the other Archibald J. Gull, and they got to taste everything that could travel in a kid's pocket. Once Marv offered Archibald an ice cream cone filled with sauerkraut, and that "flying Dutchman" from Tawas Bay relished it to the last shred.

The kids were always "trying the gulls out" to see what they'd eat, or wouldn't eat. Vic once blew a precious penny on a shoestring of black licorice. As was their custom in feeding the gulls, the kids would take a bite and then break off a piece for the gulls. Vic broke a big piece off for himself, and then a little piece for Archibald. (Vic was like that when he was a kid, he liked the big pieces best.) Archibald took a bite, downed it quickly; Vic took another

147

big bite, and impatiently Archibald grabbed the rest of the licorice shoestring, about a yard long—and flew out across the bay toward Charity Island, with the black shoestring dangling from his mouth. Vic thought it was hilarious fun, but I couldn't share his merriment . . . told him I was afraid Archibald might, somehow, get it wrapped around his neck and not be able to get it off. Vic worried about that gull for two or three days when he didn't show up. A couple mornings, real early before his usual getting-up time, he was down at the beach in his pajamas calling plaintively: "Come back again, Archibald!" The gull came back, glided into the white sand on the beach from Charity Island way, like he'd never been away. After that, no more shoestring licorice ever went to the beach. Once, with the aid of saliva, Marv pasted a "Red Hot Dollar," a jujy-fruit type of candy, on Archibald's head, pasted it tenderly and firmly in place. The next day when the gull came back, he was still wearing his red hat. With capitalistic prowess, the kids reasoned it was: "One dollar that had gone a long way."

Once when I sat on the beach absorbed in sober thoughts—was probably worrying about my doctor bill or what food in the cheap realm might occur on the Girard supper table, when an eerie, half-human cry penetrated the air. A pair of gulls, white as a bride's festooning, white as an egg shampoo, loomed against the sky. Round and round in faultless grace they reeled, with the slow measures of an old-world minuet.

Loud and hysterical were their bickerings, like twelve women debating in a jury room. Coloratura sopranos they were, so high they could have used Yma Sumac for a tuning fork. They swept low over the jade-green water, and the underparts of their bodies caught up the reflections of the translucent green, making them an exquisite pair of jade-green birds—an exquisite sight I have never been privileged to see again.

There are folks who declare with vehemence that they dislike gulls with a true vengeance. They dislike their raucous screaming and their "gluttony way of eating." I'll bet those people never lived on a farm and beheld a threshing crew at work 'round the family board. Those human gulls really knew subtraction.

The folks who do not like seagulls are probably the same ones who dislike the ponderous stretches of northern Michigan, known as "Skiberian plains." They are those rambling acres and acres of fruitless soil, tattooed with scrub oaks and scrubby jack pines, that abound in the northern Lower Peninsula of Michigan. To be sure, they are not the things of woodland architecture that might be desired. But like the cactus of Arizona or the sagebrush of Nevada, they are symbolic. They struggle on untiringly through the years, stunted and emaciated, waging a triumphal challenge where other vegetation passes up the banner for a mere existence. A futile life, but certainly proven survivors of the fittest.

Here, too, charred stumps loom up on every hand in all shapes and sizes—like miniature battleships, wigwams, temples, igloos, or most anything. They are the grim aftermaths of the dread crimson poacher, those mad forest fires that tell their tales too well.

The area around Tawas Bay still tells its history well. Much of the area along the highway leading into Tawas City from the south is still covered with huge pine stumps—which, in their days, must have been towering cathedral pines. In some places the stumps are so close together, the land remains as pasture land. The areas under farm cultivation indicate fertile fields with ages of leaves and pine needles under their porous loam. I have seen seagulls follow along the freshly-plowed furrows scrounging for some delectable earthworms. An unforgettable sight was a seagull perched on the handles of a walking plow the farmer had left in the field. The gull was perched there patiently, sitting and looking, as if waiting for the farmer to resume his plowing again.

In some places on Tawas Bay may still be seen remnants of the old lumbering docks. They were left there when the timbering era was concluded—and eventide, high-tide and riptide have left nothing but weathered footings enduring along the shoreline. And rather pretty they are, too, in a crude, homely sort of way—and depending how you look at things. We're back to the preacher and the spittin' Boy Scout looking at the Grand Canyon again, and each seeing something entirely different.

Several years ago, the Kiwanians of Michigan dedicated their first planting of Norway pines in Huron National Forest, in the "land of the Tawases"—Tawas City and East Tawas. It was the largest reforesting project ever sponsored in the country, when 5,777 of Michigan's idle acres were planted.

It was a united effort of all Kiwanis clubs in Michigan, and meant the plowing of furrows of 5,000 miles in length, and the planting of seven million seedlings that first year.

They made up their minds that the days of speech-making and writing were over, that something constructive should be done with those idle acres spilling over northern Michigan in the Au Sable River country. They got the Federal authorities to help finance the project, and a September Arbor Day was on its way. The dedication services were on the rostrum of the McCullom Banks, the same McCullom Banks that formed the famous log rollway in the timber days. The harvest of a winter's cutting for miles and miles around was accumulated at the banks, and early springtime found the skidways loosened, and virgin white and Norway pines went toppling, heaving and swaying into the swelling Au Sable River. Riverboys, stripped down to their cardinal nether garments and seagoing boots with vicious calks, mounted the backs of the raw timbers and piloted them to their "pockets."

Often it was fair sailing, with never a mutiny in the vast yellow and white population. Then again came log tumults on the troubled water. Atmosphere and footing were turned to a white wake by splashing water—as the

150

Beautiful they are—in a crude, homely sort of way—
remnants of old lumbering docks at Tawas Bay, Michigan.

riverboys, supple and ambidextrous, jumped from one log to another to release the tangled logs.

Often the bark of the logs was loosened in the exciting game of liquid battledore. Greased lightning was pretzel-coated compared to a kingly pine without its overcoat. It was a prize riverboy, indeed, who could ride a whole season through without the catch phrase: "duckin' of his lifetime."

The Tawas country was timber country. The timber barrens created by timber barons are being replaced. The Kiwanians followed their first planting the following year with another 5,000-acre planting. The grown trees are there today in the Huron National Forest, filled with get-up and go, and still "growin' like weeds."

. . . The ice going off Tawas Bay that first springtime we knew it was memorable. Day after day, the water covered the ice and froze over again. One after another, the iceboats came ashore and went into drydock. Far out in the middle of the bay, ice was exhausted, like most of us on the shore, after a long endless winter. The old-timers looked that way and chewed their tobacco a little harder. One would have thought there was some invisible, mechanical hookup so harmoniously did their jaws work. "It won't be long now!" they knew from experience.

The "bite of the bay" still claimed its own. Here, the ice always came first and stayed the longest. Bite of the bay, indeed! The bite of Zeus, it was, the old storm God in person. That winter never wanted to give up. Some of the gulls came ashore and trekked the frozen sand. Others sailed on outstretched wings searching the deep . . . on . . . always on. Aloof and voiceless. Restless birds in the wayward winds.

. . . Came warming springtime, and the kids used their big toes for making pictures in the white sands of the beach. The gulls flew by to see what the kids were doing. I used to sit on the beach with my arms akimbo, or something like that, and watch the waves build up. With my head poised still like a taxidermist's owl, I could sit and watch for hours. Once I saw the waves get angry and angrier, and it was not a pretty sight. They were neither blue nor green, neither periwinkle nor heliotrope—just a terrible, monstrous, sickening yellow. Great hungry waves, high as the fish houses on the shore, coming thick and fast as flying words.

I thought one day as I watched them create their tumult in broad daylight that we humans in a manner are all sailors, really. It's the troubled waters that prove our undoing.

I wondered as I watched an angry tumult of the waves on Tawas Bay just how we humans must appear in an angry mood. Unkind words, bits of unfairness . . . hoarded malice . . . past grievances. How would we feel if the contents of our minds were suddenly tumbled out in a heap for all the big gawking world to see? Yeah . . . Just how would we feel?

## THE BALLAD OF A MICHIGAN 'JACK

I'm a shanty boy from Tawas Bay
    And I'm six feet one in socks;
I'm cut proud across the galluses
    And my fists are hard like rocks.
My cant hook ranks with the best of them,
    I'm king of the Michigan bush,
And I won't take much from any man
    In the way of a verbal push.

I've turned away from the wild north wind
    When my whiskered face was raw,
Still, from sun to sun, I've labored on . . .
    There was pine to chop and saw.

153

## Blow for Batten's Crossing!

I've broken jams at the river's bend,
    I've danced the darting log;
I've slept and slaved in a pine-tree world
    That would set your heart agog.

I've sent the blade of my eager axe
    To the heart of a sky-high spruce;
I've felt it shudder and then go down,
    It was like all Hell broke loose!
I've stood there in the after-dust
    And heard the sawyer's call;
Those burly lads would share my tree,
    But it was I who made it fall.

I've wooed and won the satin girls
    Of booming Saginaw;
I've roared in whiskey palaces
    And got my face stomped raw.
Then back to camp as best I could,
    Broke and battle-weary,
To lick my wounds and curse the likes
    Of Hansen and O'Leary.

I've swung my boots with awkward grace
    To a bunkhouse fiddler's reel;
I've sung the songs of rivermen
    In a style not quite genteel.
When the bunks were piled with snoring men
    I've slipped the earthly bars;
Alone at last, in my mackinaw,
    I'd smoke and count the stars.

I've worked the woods till it all went stale,
    Till I sulked at the daily ration;
Oh! the oaths I hurled at those shanty cooks
    Were filled with Irish passion!

## Come Back Again, Archibald

I've used up all my tender years
   Following the timber rush;
From the Straits down to Au Sable way
   I've spoiled the forest's hush.

But I wouldn't swap the old tote road
   For a screaming thoroughfare;
I'd miss the boys and the smell of pine
   In the early morning air.
So belly up, you husky 'jacks,
   Or you'll get my boots in time;
Drink long and hearty of the red
   And hear this logger's rhyme.

I'm a shanty boy from Tawas Bay
   And I'm six feet one in socks;
I'm cut proud across the galluses
   And my fists are hard like rocks.
The "Iosco Kid," that's how I'm known,
   And boys, you'll all agree . . .
With hands like these and shoulders broad,
   A lumberjack I'll be!
         —*Marvin Eugene Girard*

# 17

# THE GOOD LAND—
# AND THE BAD TIMES

ON DAD'S 65TH BIRTHDAY, HE CLIMBED TO the top of the windmill at the Home Place. He had climbed it on his 64th birthday, on his 63rd birthday, the 62nd, the 61st, and right down the line to when he had first gotten the windmill. It was the only windmill around, and Dad was as proud of it as he was of his expensive Hamilton pocket watch in its engraved gold case. He wound that watch at exactly the same time every night, just before he went to bed, and caressingly held it to his forehead to hear its faultless ticking. That watch was a heavy timepiece, heavy as a rutabaga, heavy as a Ben Davis apple.

The purpose of going upstairs on the windmill, it seems, was to oil it. It must have had a lot of places on it that required lubrication, because he always stayed and stayed up there. It was like he was going to school.

We never figured out how he could be oiling something and gawking around so much. Must have been some powerful pretty sights from atop that windmill, 35 feet off the ground. The climbing of the windmill on his birthday each year, it seemed, was a birthday present to himself.

He'd shinny up the ladder of the windmill like a red squirrel climbing an oak tree, sure-footed as a mountain-climber scaling the Matterhorn. Fiddle! the clumsy-footed kids who couldn't stand up straight on a little patch of ice certainly had no business getting ten feet off the ground.

None of us, however, ever got to see what the panorama up there might be because windmill-climbing had definitely been off limits for the kids down through the years. And certainly Mother was well enough acquainted with all the sights and all the work shenanigans of the farm without doing a perch act to get an air-view of the place.

Dad, who had been deaf all the years we kids could remember, said he could hear better up there atop the windmill. He also heard better around the threshing machines. He didn't have to see lips move to hear then, he actually got all messages "by ear."

Mother said once "that boy oughta build himself a tree house up there." That was once, I believe, during a slight altercation of the Batten household—another cool, cold war that had temporarily besieged the nile green house at the crossing.

If Dad thought Mother was "puttery" about some of her household stints, like making time-consuming artistic designs on top of her famous butter prints, she thought he sure knew all the ways and means of dodging things he didn't like to do. Milking cows was one of those things. Mother said he was a "sloppy milker," and he was sloppy because he just didn't like to milk cows, and used his sloppiness as a way out of an undesirable task.

When he milked, he got his pant legs wet from the knees to the bottoms of them. He got his shoes completely covered with milk spatters. His shoes were fully integrated long before Supreme Court edicts for humanity. The cats always gathered 'round when he milked because they knew he wasn't too adept at hitting the milk pail on target. They'd gather 'round his milk stool like colonists around a new Betsy Ross flag.

Dad told us once he could hear the cow's heart beating when he was milking, and, of course, we didn't believe it till we tried it ourselves. The feat was very elementary, and entirely true. You simply put your forehead against the cow's flank and, sure enough, that bovine heart ticks right along. The steady pulse, the rhythm of the fingers as they caress the bovine keyboard, and the swish-swish of the stream of milk to the pail, builds a camaraderie between the cow and the milker that is peaceful and understanding. Cows know the people who hate to milk them, they can spot them immediately. Dad was never on the Hit Parade of any cow in the barnyard. He'd rather clean stables, curry the horses, or feed a freshly-weaned calf by the finger method than siphon the offerings of a surmising cow with mutiny on her mind. Mother said he never did learn to "strip" a cow properly, so the net result was he left it for those who could do it better.

But the windmill oiling was his project. And his alone. And he always did it on his birthday, like a ritual. Maybe he was testing himself to see if he could do it as easily as he had the year before. He never hurried down—he was busy looking toward the creek flats, toward the good land and the good Jersey cows on the hills, and the long winding lane with its rail fencing, and the clumps of pin cherry trees growing along the wayside.

Mother's birthdays came and went. In modern day parlance, they would best be described as: "No big deal!" In fact, Mother chose to forget them entirely. All of them. Those past, and those coming up. With so many in the family, it was difficult to remember sometimes how old everyone was on the birthday currently up. One of the kids once asked Mother how old she was that birthday. And real, real quick-like came back the answer: "Old enough to know better!"

159

Then came a kid's inevitable question right back to the quick answer: "Know better than what?"

A question like that was always the wrong question to ask Mother. She just had too many answers to it. And they were all good answers. She didn't have to excavate the reservoirs of her memory to bring them to the surface. They were right there handy, browned on the fire, and dying to be turned over. And she could turn them over, too, real deftly—and with the same matchless vigor and agility she could turn over a buttermilk pancake "done" on the Kalamazoo wood range, with pine knots supplying the fuel for the occasion.

Oh, foolish, foolish kids—how asinine can you be? You know so very little, and have so very much to learn. You subteen-age kids with your fresh physiognomies and your broad grinny grins with youthful pearly teeth always airing, don't ask Johannah Batten how old she is, and what she knows about life. She knows all the chapters about it—and learned too much, too soon. She feels much older than she really is, and isn't about to tell what she knows. That would take all night, and all the nights for the rest of the week to tell it all. It wouldn't be good listenin' and you wouldn't want to hear it.

How do you tell young daughters about the awful heaviness of an unborn child; how do you tell them about the dozens of nights your swollen feet and legs hurt too much to permit sleep; how do you tell them that bearing ten children isn't the same as green apple diarrhea? . . . You don't tell them. You don't tell them about the midwives who knew all about births supposedly, but sometimes not quite enough. And you don't tell them about having twins and doing it the lonely way—real lonely, and scary way, when even the fearless midwife got scared and ran away from the complexity of it all. Their dad was away at the lumber camp, and you waited. Alone.

She isn't going to tell about the passing of little Freddie at the age of seven years from scarlet fever, the youngster between George and Ida. And she isn't going to tell about that awful summer night when 16-year-old Johnny—carefree, laughing, fun-loving Johnny effervescing with the duration of boyhood, went swimming on a hot summer's night after supper with some other lads in a nearby lake, and was drowned. He had screamed and coaxed for help, with a smile on his face, and they thought he was kidding them—they thought he was only foolin' them to see if they'd come and get him . . . and was drowned in Little Lake, surrounded with the same kind of woods that were in the nearby creek flats.

Tearless Mother changed a great deal after the loss of Johnny. She became very withdrawn, and scolded a lot. She quilted in silence; she made corn tassles as decorations on her butter prints, in silence—she designed oak leaves and thistle blooms, and they were the prettiest designs she'd ever made; she planted flowers till her flower garden was bulging with blossoms; she made a vegetable garden that was big enough for three hungry families. She gently scratched the soil around the wild honeysuckles, the wild roses and the woods' violets in silence. So tenderly did she scratch the porous soil it seemed she was massaging it. For years, Dad had done the same thing every time he stopped the prancing horses for a "rest" in the field. He'd always pick up a handful of soil from the open furrow and rub and rub it through his fingers from one hand to the other as if it had a therapeutic quality. He always did it whether he sat on the stubble ground by the fence row or atop the rail fence with a couple bob-whites. It was good, good land, and he liked being very close to it. And besides, one can be very silent sifting dirt through the fingers. You don't have to talk—you don't have to think . . . just a tablespoon of good land in the hollow of the hand. And you!

No, kids, Mother isn't going to tell you about the wolves in the woods she remembers, and she certainly isn't going to tell you about those at the back door. They came often, much too often. Dad through the years had often kidded about them, but Mother couldn't—the hurt was still too near.

Dad, too, missed Johnny a great deal. He had been named after Dad, and possessed much of Dad's same temperament. The oldest son, George, had been gone from home for several years, and Dad relished having another masculine figure around the home. John was an avid reader of the daily newspaper like Dad, and already had acquired a voluble knowledge of the workings of the Land of the Free and the Home of the Careless Cash, and like John 1st before him was equally opinionated. Dad liked that: the ready mind, the intelligent mind with galloping humor. It was a velvet glove approach with rose "pickers" all over the gloves; it was a smooth, buttery kind of thrust with a harpoon on the business end of the verbal missile. He was a stand-up comedian sitting down across the table from Dad and exchanging banter. He was a youthful Will Rogers without a rope, without a platform.

After Johnny's death, Dad worked in the fields as long as it was daylight, and even the horses were ready to call it a day. Dad complained about feeling "gimpy" in the middle of the afternoon, and Mother started sending a fresh eggnog to the fields for him. She taught the kids how to make an eggnog: cold milk from the root house, a beaten egg, a little sugar, a spot of vanilla and a pinch of freshly-grated nutmeg. Always, she used a fresh egg, some of them still warm from their late entry into the nest. Mother would often call to one of the kids: "Is there ere an egg in the hen house?" We kids, bratty kids that some of us were, would sometimes mimic her Irish brogue. We didn't like it—thought she should speak good English like all the other women in the neighborhood, good-sounding English like we were learning in school. In due time, Mother overcame her Irish brogue—and I'm sure the other kids missed it, too, even though they never admitted it. We should have had a few trips to the woodshed, laid over the sawbuck and gotten a good scutching on the you-know-where. Mother was too kind to us . . . you have to grow up and have kids of your own to really smarten up and learn things.

A lot of water has gone over the dam, under the gate, up the river and over the lea—and people haven't been climbing windmills for years and years. Dad had never allowed us kids to climb the windmill or linger around when farmers brought their nutsy cows to visit our Jersey bull, Jasper. We were always sent on an urgent chore somewhere else. Mother had never killed our spirits by nagging at us too much. She nagged just enough to be the right amount—so we didn't pick our noses, so the girls discreetly crossed their knees, spoke softly and didn't chatter like magpies.

We were never told about the birds and bees, guess the folks thought we were passably bright kids and should have been doing a little homework around the farm in the way of observing what was going on around the premises: roosters and hens, the cows and Jasper, the ram and the ewes, Thomas J. Cat and Priscilla. We had seen all kinds of babies—barn swallows, wrens, robins, meadow larks, orioles, chickens, guinea hens, calves, lambs, kittens, squirrels and rabbits, and we didn't find them in a rain barrel.

All the eight kids married, and Dad and Mother were always happy with the in-laws annexed to the family. Four grandsons and ten granddaughters. More girls, girls, girls!

There had been many times down through the years when the kids had the idea that probably Dad and Mother were a pair of misfits, and never should have married. They were totally unlike. They had equal capacity for love of the land, love of animals, and the inherent love of the kids. Dad had a lot of shanty boy on his tongue; Mother had a lot of County Cork on hers till the bratty kids shamefully Americanized most of it out of her. Dad thought Mother lacked a sense of humor; Mother thought Dad had no patience. Dad thought Mother was too prudent and

Photo by H. Girard

Sex education—country-style

frugal; Mother thought Dad was a galloping spendthrift. Dad liked politics and the workings of the Government; Mother lost much of her appreciation of the Government when they eliminated her free garden seeds.

Like Champ and Jess, the best horses that ever lived on the Batten farm, they always pulled together best, it seemed, when the going was the toughest.

18

# "SILVER JACK"
# WAS ONE OF THEM

MY DAD, JACK BATTEN—"SILVER JACK OF THE Rollways," would have loved the Michigan Lumberjack Monument in Huron National Forest in memory of her shanty boys, those other days "way back when" the wealth of the state was measured by her timbered acres and saw-mills instead of automobile factories.

Michigan history will never again record such a migration to the wilds as took place each year when thousands of wilderness-taming lumberjacks teemed into the camps. Them days have gone forever, grammar and all! It was the pine yesteryear in Michigan. By the hundreds and more hundreds, they came. It wasn't a boy's work, but work for straight-backed, sturdy-bodied and man-grown forest warriors. They were a conglomerate aggregation: towering Swedes; stocky, black-eyed Frenchmen—cussed and cussing; broguish burring Scotchmen; Canadian Irishmen with big feet and good stories; Johnny Bulls with their bloody, bloomin' suavity; Yankee doodles and Yankee dandies.

ERECTED TO PERPETUATE THE MEMORY OF THE
PIONEER LUMBERMEN OF MICHIGAN THROUGH
WHOSE LABORS WAS MADE POSSIBLE THE
DEVELOPMENT OF THE PRAIRIE STATES

### MICHIGAN's LUMBERJACK MONUMENT
located on the High Rollways of the Au Sable River.

They had muscles for life, and there was work to be done. "All that out there" was to be cut down and hauled away to the mill. Trees to be conquered and vanquished, and their sawdust innards to bleed on the forest floors. The plutocratic pines were going "to spill their guts" for civilization.

They tramped into camp with their gear on their gallused backs, or their skimpy allotment of sartorial belongings done up in a straw valise with a rope tied around its middle. Usually their belongings arrived in a printed grain bag or burlap sack hanging over their shoulder blades. They didn't come by plane, car or bus, they tramped down the tote-road on "Shank's ponies" and the ponies were dammified tired. Their bodies were desperate for nourishment and their weary feet wanted out of their shoe pacs. The traveler wanted food, employment and rest, and pronto-like, in that order. He'd get the job first and ask about the price paid afterward.

No questions were asked—where had he worked previously? What was his educational background? . . . What was his Social Security number? . . . Did he carry Blue Cross insurance? He was put to work where men were needed the most, and the "straw boss" would find out soon enough where he belonged.

Some of the young "whipper-snappers" never made it to camp, if some of the old-hands got to them first. They'd tell the young guys "not dry behind the ears" that it was sure one hell of a place to work. And they'd go into their spiel of what a dangerous place it was to be around. "Them danged gillaloue birds often get a guy the very first day," they'd tell the wood's greenhorn. The gillaloue bird, so their story went, never took up residence anywhere but near a lumber camp. They laid square eggs and were the laziest bird that ever laid an egg. They'd use their nest for an outhouse and when it got filled to capacity would just move on and steal the nest of another gillaloue bird that was a better housekeeper. They were, it seems, the original "dirty bird."

There was no tree in all the woods a lumberjack hated to fall quite as much as a tree that was filled with nests of dozens of gillaloue birds. And if you happened to be in the woods and looking up at the sky and a gillaloue bird flew over—and they never, never were potty-trained, and you happened to be hit in the eye, you were a goner for sure. Blinded for life, right on the spot, before you could get to camp and have the eye washed out. It happened every day, so their story went.

Many a young recruit to the lumber camp never got to the office door to get hired. He never got further than the spot in the tote-road where the old-timers gave out with their Audubon wisdom. He'd drop the pack off his back and high-tail it back over the tote-road in the direction from which he'd come. And the old-timers laughed and laughed their brown-toothed grins at the athletic sprinting of the young gaffer, and would chomp off another generous bite of plug-cut tobacco from their pockets—glad to have had a good laugh to loosen up their day.

Even if the raw recruits escaped the gillaloue bird scare, or the scare about the "widow-maker" trees that were everywhere, the way ahead for them was always rough for the first couple weeks. The widow-maker tree scare was worse than the gillaloue bird scare. They were the trees that had been cut and hadn't fallen properly but had become lodged against other trees on the way down, and refused all efforts at being budged. But just turn your back, and unexpectedly, they'd come crashing down on their own accord. Downright treacherous, they were, I-gollys! and a couple guys "got it" nearly every day, according to the old-timers. And it always seemed it got a guy with a whole houseful of little young'n's, and snuffed him out before he could stammer: "Pa-Pa-Paul Bun-Bunyan!" . . . "A lot of danged pretty widows around," the old fellows groaned. Occasionally, it seemed, the scourge of the woods—a gillaloue bird tree with its dozens of reeking, wretching, odorous-smelling nests, would also become a widow-maker. It was a double-header catastrophe when that calamity happened, the dreaded tragedy of the lumber camp. It evoked a nostril-repelling odor that could be smelled all the way to the chuckhouse. It came in through the doors like a gusty wind; it permeated the timbers and the heavy clothes. Sometimes the powerful, pervading odor was even too much for the gillaloue birds themselves and they flew away to other camps many miles away where the woods were clean and piney. The story grew in magnitude each time the old-timers repeated it.

Camp initiations when every newcomer to camp was admitted to the Royal Order of Shanty Boys were big occasions. They took place after "fat pork and sundown" or suppertime in our vernacular. The initiated rendered some conception of art in the way of singing, jigging or fiddling. The high-hat fellow who wouldn't buddy up with the rest of the shanty boys soon felt his self-importance shrink to instant humility. He was bound to receive a barrage of shoe pacs, antiquated eggs, cabbage heads, rutabagas, anything or everything in sight. Jonah, Howard-Johnsoning in the whale, had a picnic compared to the serenading accorded a high-hat, greenhorn shanty boy.

Seemed like a greenhorn shanty boy, especially a high-hat one, had so very much to learn. He graduated downward to the rank of "Moss back" by the end of the first week. Out in the woods, he got a good liberal education. After a few galloping trips back to camp to "fetch real quick" a three-bitted axe or a left-handed canthook, he learned there were no such implements. Indoors, he learned that shanty boys didn't puny around with their food at the table—they just filled their faces and shut up! They didn't sleep in night shirts; they don't hog the conversation; and contrary to opinion, they never, never bad-mouthed the women folks.

Far, far into the night, winter winds swept the forests

171

and swayed the patriarchal trees. Timber wolves bayed like prairie coyotes. At times, it was the plaintive call of a lone wolf entreating his gray clan for a hunt. He would point his nose at a star and howl the woes and cadences of his departed ancestors, dead and dust. Then again, most mournful dirge of a wilderness night, would come the blood-thirsty call of the pack. Closer and ever closer, or further and further away, their requiem cries floated on wings of the gypsy winds. Wild cats catapulted as only those cats can pult, and white-tailed deer leisurely smacked up the wisps of hay around the stable doors. A seasoned shanty boy could tell the exact instant when a timber wolf brought down his prey. Always, always they went for the throat where life was near the surface. There was the last triumphal howl. Then silence.

Indoors, the dog-tired, bone-weary shanty boys pounded their ears. They snored to Morpheus in all the keys of the musical scale, and the very rafters of the bunkhouse seemed to hang in the balance. Pack rats, fearless and investigative, were up and doing. They were better known as trade rats— they could trade with the camp's most-reputed, epicurean tightwad and beat him at his own game. Soo woolen sox were stealthily carried away and replaced with Norway splinters. A penny cedar lead pencil might be replaced with a corncob pipe from the opposite end of the bunk-house. Many a towering lumberjack screamed a raucous yelp in the morning when he inserted a foot into a shoe pac and found that a family of rodents had taken up squatter's homesteading.

Perhaps back in their kidhood days, everyone of them had heard the oft-related tale of Bruce and the courageous spider that goaded him to unstinted victory, or perhaps they had marveled at the agility with which a roach clambers up a wall, crosses the ceiling, and gallops down the opposite wall. But many a full-grown shanty boy, powerful and in-destructible, performed equivalent antics while a pack rat whittled nonchalantly at his ears.

Mornings came while the sleepers were still snoring and fretfully tossing their heads on the blue-ticked pillows. Seemed, usually, they had just gotten to sleep when the lusty-lunged chore boy, with the vocal capacity of a hog-caller from Ioway, would fling open the door of the bunkhouse and bellow: "Roll out, boys, roll out! 'Twill soon be daylight 'nd the tote road's so full of snow that daylight can't get in here. Roll out! ROLL OUT!" It was downright disgusting how jovial, how-bright-with-all-their-might the shanty cooks could be so early in the mornings. Filled with banter and enthusiasm for the new day, they knew they were Gabriels right in the kitchen. They knew full well the work gotten out of the boys would depend on the grub that went into them. It was "chuck that stuck to the ribs" they created, food with stamina and amperage that would have put intestinal fortitude in a big bad wolf or a buzzard.

The boys all had heavy-duty appetites. The exact instant Paddy McGraw or "Beany" Stevens appeared in the doorway, flour sack dish towels tossed over a shoulder, to give the summons of "Mushay! Mushay! Mushay!" there was a terrific scramble for seating room. They sat down to a rough board table that was sure the Grand Rapids of the pine world. They bracketed their ample feet securely to the splintery plank floor and lit out after old-fashioned calories. Every meal was Thanksgiving. Mountains of cabbage and pig knuckles; heaps of fat pork; mounds of potatoes; beans and more beans in squadrons and platoons; whole regiments of cakes and molasses cookies. And Johnny cake, yellow as cowslips and happy as dandelion blow. They ate pie after pie without getting pious, and bushels of warmed-over mush. And there was shanty cake, oh yes! the supreme delicacy of the chuckhouse. It was a rich concoction, patterned after a biscuit recipe, and baked in mammoth black dripping pans. It wasn't meant to be cut, but like sponge cake or bologna, was at its best when broken off in hunks. And a generous hunk of shanty cake dunked into a giant mug of black coffee as you ate along was something pretty hard to beat. I-gollys, if it wasn't! The coffee was tall, dark and rugged. It had power and glory behind it, and assorted abrasive qualities ahead of it.

Each day, each week, each winter month followed the same pattern. The sleep dust was out of the jack's eyes crazy-early each morning; they had stretched their weary muscles and found elastic sinews for a new day. The horses were ready; the men were ready; the trees were ready. There was too much readiness always. And came the year, and so suddenly it seemed, it was all over. Mostly all over. No longer were the pines so thick the sun rays could not penetrate to the ground beneath. There was no mistake about it—the landlookers could see it, the old-timers could see it; even a greenhorn recruit with faulty vision could have noticed it.

The colorful pine days were nearing a sad termination. Already, it was noticed, there had been too much subtraction, and no addition. Some of the more adventurous jacks went to Washington and Oregon. The slaying of the big trees had taken a certain hold on them that pulled like a magnet. It was a challenge they could not refuse—like men following gold, like a dog chasing a cat, like a pot following a rainbow. Many of the boys remained in Michigan to continue the harvesting of the hardwood and hemlock forests. Lumberjacks declare with vehemence there's something about the smell of pine that you never forget. Its distinctive aroma takes hold like the grip on a cabin latch. A kingly pine, it seems, is an imperial thing even in death—that last fatal lurch he takes with royal abandon, always a plutocrat to the last!

Perhaps the reluctant part in reviewing the archives of yesterday is that the timbers were thinned in the first place almost to the point of devastation. We hear criticism so often of the timber barons who made timber barrens—of the "timber hogs" whose ruthless axes and saws knew no mercy; who had no regard for such a thing as primeval

174

forests, and saw instead only the dollars and dollars represented in those timbered acres.

And yet, after all, it is quite easy to understand how it must have looked to those lumbering magnates in those days. Stretched out before them, in four directions, were those limitless acres of venerable trees. Pines especially so thick they seemed gasping for air. Maples standing shoulder to shoulder, erect and reverent, like some day they might sing "The Star Spangled Banner" before a Tiger ballgame. They thought it was a sight, a commodity that would last forever. It was a day of jubilant plenty, and timbering like gold-digging had been in '49, was merely a game of "dog eat dog." They never reasoned how long it would take for a sapling to reach maturity. It was long before "Conservation" was on the statute books, and folks didn't know anymore about it than coffee boiling over knows about "seein' the world."

Today finds Michigan in a widely different role—painstakingly conserving her natural resources and putting forth every endeavor to make her prolific acres sparkle as gems of Vacationland. She has the sky-blue waters; each year she is getting more dark green pines, as is evidenced by the repeated plantings in her National forests of the state. And verdant thanks to the creators of the idea for her Lumberjack Monument, we have a tribute to the boys who followed the tote-roads, and watched the neutral population eddying downstream in the Au Sable to found a nation—the Au Sable, the river that conceived more raw footage of lumber than any other river in the world.

Robert Aitken, noted New York sculptor, wisely chose a lithe Schandanavian as a principle of his presentation. A peavey, clinched in his fists in "do or die" fashion, the young Thor stands ready to do his derndest. A landlooker is there, standing in a calculating pose, as if pondering the scale of that master pine in the distance. And the sawyer, too, is there, by Jox! ready to do his sawdust. Twenty tons of cut granite were required for the base of the monument;

175

Au Sable's "High Rollways" where winter's logs
were piled awaiting the coming of spring.

the intricate sculptoring is a two-ton bronze casting. Dedicated in 1932, the $50,000 monument stands in Huron National Forest, 200 feet above the Au Sable River, where the historic Thompson Tote Trail emerges to meet the river—the Indian's picture river, named by them, and meaning "The river of sandy bottom."

There are only a few of the seasoned sourdoughs left who tamped the icy tote-roads in the resinous days when timber was plutocrat in Michigan. They have left this mortal coil and gone to a roistering Valhalla where they hobnob with the cowpunchers, the fur traders, Indian fighters, the gold prospectors and the Gloucester fisherman.

My Dad, "Silver Jack of the Rollways," would have loved that Lumberjack Monument. Called "Silver Jack" because of the white wake made by his calked boots when he churned the waters of the Au Sable to a silver froth as he fearlessly jumped from one log to another, and rode the vortex of Au Sable's foam to the End of the Trail.

# 19

# BACK WHERE I CAME FROM

WHEN YOU GROW UP WITH GREEN SOD UNDER
your feet instead of concrete, you have a distinct sense of
values that "comes with the package." You haven't been
raised with the idea that work is all for fools and horses,
and that money will raise you far beyond the necessity of
vulgar toil.

Everybody worked back where I came from. Horses
put their necks to the collar and their strong hips to the
whiffletrees; Dad put his sinews to the hoe, the pitchfork
and the sickle; Mother, doing her housework, meandered
through a houseful of miscellaneous sized kids—antsy-
pantsy young'n's, always squirming, always gabbing, always hungry. Daily, she put her sanity in the hands of her
benevolent Maker. When her brain got exhausted and her
courage bogged, her hands would get busy. She'd whack
the butter "print" a few resounding whacks with the butter
ladle and it sounded like another trip to the cedar shingles

Photo by H. Girard

When you grow up with green sod under your feet
instead of concrete, you have a
distinct sense of values that "comes with the package."

and the woodshed; she'd knit a few inches on the long black stockings that would be going to school next winter; she'd baste the hem in a dress for long-legged H. B. that had been handed down from Beulah, and that had been handed down to her from Amy. All dresses got a long reign of sovereignity before being relegated to the rag basket to be made into rag rugs. Eli Whitney would have been happy to have known his cotton gin made possible such long-wearing calico. The only way to interrupt the long tenure of a hand-me-down dress was to be a hit-and-run victim with the barbed wire fence, and have the dress become an immediate casualty. That always worked.

Kids who went to school back there ate pretty much the same kind of fare from their lunch pails that we did. Sometimes "sody biscuits," biscuits that had been left over from supper the night before. You can't get too hoity-toity eating cold sody biscuits, regardless of how you spell it. And cold buttermilk Johnny cake reminded you that it tasted better when it was hot.

Mother was always thoughtful about biscuits and Johnny cake. She usually planned the baking of them so there'd be none of them left over—just enough, maybe, so there'd be a taste of them for our old dog, Prince. Mother planned her bread-baking so there'd always be bread for sandwiches, and she hadn't lived around a passel of mouthy kids and not learned they weren't stalwarts of either cold biscuits or Johnny cake in their lunch pails. I can't recall that Mother ever inflicted cold pancakes on our lunch pails. Many of the kids at school did carry cold pancakes, and had a small jar of dark Caro syrup or some homemade jam to go on top of them. The Indian kids often brought huge pancakes, and used them as a jacket wrapped around their smoked brook trout. The kids said they were wonderful, and it was one thing in their lunch pails that would never be traded. Not even for a mammoth Northern Spy apple, a raspberry jam sandwich and a piece of vinegar pie all put together. None of us ever got to know the gastronomical delight of what a smoked Au Sable brook trout with a pancake overcoat wrapped around it would taste like.

Pancakes were usually the "in" thing for breakfast. Ex-lumberjacks never talked about their mother's cooking— they always bragged about the delectable concoctions the shanty cook conjured up. Always they wanted pancackes for breakfast, lean side pork and sop, fried potatoes and pie, if available. Dad liked his pancakes with heavy sweet cream and sugar on top of them. No little triangles of toast for him and a peasley-size cup of coffee. He wanted coffee in his pint-size moustache cup, and the Leghorn rooster could have the toast. And he wasn't too crazy about it either, but it made a nice corsage to take a busty lady-love pullet who'd been shining her green eyes in his direction out in the chicken yard.

Dad wanted his coffee danky dark, with power and glory behind it. He wanted coffee with authority and deter-mination—that could rear back on its caffeine heels and head off all other beverages at the pass. Mother never al-lowed us kids to drink coffee till we were in the 8th grade, said it would stunt our growth. And it probably would have. You can't swallow lightning. When we got to be 8th graders, we graduated to coffee—half and half, that is, half coffee and half milk. Made you think of your pacifier days.

Bread pudding must have been another chuckhouse goodie because Dad liked it often. And he wanted plenty of big seeded raisins in it, and they looked like big limpid, black eyes staring up at you from the deep cereal dish. One couldn't get too hoity-toity eating bread pudding, either— you knew dern well it was made from the "scrap bread" that had been left on the plates at mealtime. It was one dessert that was bound to keep you humble.

Dad and Mother never broke our spirits by giving us too much work. We were given enough to know we were expected to help carry the family load. We weren't told with apology: "Now, child, this is all for your own good." We were told with cool, cold, deliberation: "You've got just ten minutes, kid, to git it done!" Dad and Mother were never wishy-washy about anything. All requests were made "crystal clear" right from the start. They made things perfectly transparent long before Nixon was heard about.

True, Mother was "short" with us on occasion, and the "occasion" was plural. But, looking back, her life was no bed of roses. There were too many beds of weeds to be "kept down" from the garden plants a-coming. Her roses were the ones she talked to, sometimes, out in the garden. Then, too, she had been pregnant more than she had been impregnated with badly-needed rest.

Neither Dad nor Mother ever told us kids that they loved us, but we were sure they did. We knew Mother loved us because she often wore her blue "wrappers" to tatters so she could buy some new flowered calico that had "just come in" at Solomon's general store, and make us some new dresses, and give us a change from the perennial hand-me downs. . . . Wonder, now, why we never once bothered to say: "Thank you." We knew she loved us because of the mustard plasters and the onion poultices she made for some of the "croupers" in the middle of the night. There was no mistake about it, Mother "knew her onions" and used them generously. Nobody ever knew exactly what went into her onion poultices, or what was left out of them, if anything. But the basic recipe went something like this: so much stewed onions, so much rye middlings, so much mustard, so much flour—all dampened with turpentine. This concoction was lavished between woolen cloths and clamped on the chest like a catcher's protector. It was supposed to have wonderful "drawing" power. Back then, things were supposed to taste and smell bad. Onion poultices didn't smell too bad, but like Dad's coffee, they had gut-power and persuasion. A half hour's wrestle with them and you cut wisdom teeth at the tender age of ten years.

Sometimes in the middle of the night, Mother would get up and make an onion souffle. 'Twas onions baked in butter, sweetened with honey, gallused with Spirits of Turpentine. One teaspoon of that potent extract and your head went amphibian; three teaspoons of it and you wilted dizzily back on the pillow and said: "Gee, Mamma, I sure wish this train wouldn't go so fast."

We knew Dad loved us because he always took time to answer the dozens of questions we threw at him. He'd stop at the end of a plowed furrow, climb up on the rail fence and lay his intelligence on the line. He knew what happened to the deer antlers that were shed in the creek flats every summer; he knew what kind of coal that Edd Boddy, the village smithy, used to keep his fire stoked so evenly. He'd tell us Paul Bunyan stories and give them a nearby locale that would roll us off the fence. Like the time, he said, Paul and his blue ox, Babe, came through our creek flats. Paul didn't try to take the mossy log that everyone else used, he thought he could easily jump across. He didn't land just right, and one of his heels dug down in the ground up to Paul's knees. And that, Dad explained, was what made that deep spring of ice cold water in the gully, with the coldest water in Alcona County. He said the first time our fractious horses, Champ and Jess, had a look at the Blue Ox that he had another run-away on his hands. That time the horses didn't stop till they got to Bryant where Charlie Cote lived. Charlie knew few people except the railroad crew. It seems that as a young man he had studied for the priesthood, had become ill, and went to northern Michigan to recuperate. He had stayed on, and spent his days in meditation, reading history and studying. He tended the water tower at Bryant that gave the little A.S.&N.W. train its daily drink.

Charlie heard the horses coming, crashing scrub oaks and jack pines off at the roots, as they tore across the "Skiberian plains." Charlie yelled something to them in French, yelled something in English, then yelled something real loud to them in French—and they stopped immediately in their tracks. He petted their noses and got them a drink of water. They nuzzled around his pockets and found some wintergreen lozenges. They quieted down completely, and he gave them a pan of grated carrots he was going to put in his pea soup that he made every day for the section hands. We never told Mother about Dad's wonderful Bunyan stories that got better and better every time he told them. We remembered too well a couple cold, silent wars that had happened in the past.

. . . Watching Ole Cherry bringing home the cows through the long winding, rail-fenced lane, was a pretty sight for a kid to remember. When you're laying belly-flop on an old wooden bridge in the creek flats and watching crabs, wily trout and green frogs, you haven't devilment on your mind. You're "living life near the core," as Thoreau put it. And no one has ever beaten the philosophy of the ole coot—the ole coot and hern guy, I mean, from Walden Pond who lived long before HUD and built himself a house for $28.12. Did it with his own industrious hot hands, by using second-hand windows and carrying second-hand barn lumber home on his back.

We kids lived life near the core for certain. And plenty of bread puddings, sody biscuits and buttermilk pancakes had kept us properly humble. We loved the hills of Home, and would always remember them. We walked to the creek flats of autumn; we belly-flopped on homemade sleds of winter and thought we were millionaire's kids; we slipped into spring with the cowslips, and the adrenalin of summer youth "pumped" our crabtree swing to the clouds.

# 20

# THE LIVING END

I HAVE LOOKED AT THE VIRGIN WHITE PINES IN the Hartwick Pines Forest (Grayling, Michigan), and each centurial pine looked like an old, old man with Trader Horn whiskers. There was a chivalry born of the Great Outdoors about them. They had seen so much life come and go—winter had followed winter; long night had followed long night, and those king pines hundreds of years old, had known weather in all its ramifications. They had known forest humidity, falling mercury, glad sunshine, and warm rains that came down in slanting strokes like the Spencerian penmanship of an old schoolmaster. Towering and lordly they were, demon demonstrators that Life paid fat dividends. Trees that had never squandered an hour or a good impulse.

And I've looked at the seedlings, newly planted, in the Huron National Forest, and thought how very much like a young baby they looked, clad only in a skimpy diaper.

They had so much growing up to do: childhood, "going up Fool's Hill" youth, adolescence, middle age and the golden years.

Aunt Tilly said one time she wished she'd never "growed up." One of the twins told her that her grammar was wrong, that she should have said "had grown up." And right back came the assertive answer: "Well, child, I have grown up enough to know I sure wish I'd never growed up!"

I have visited the old hills of Home and, somehow, the High Chaparallos of my youth didn't look nearly as big as I had remembered them. I have visited the creek flats, and the creek seemed much bigger than I had remembered it. It seemed to me, as a kid, we could spit across it anywhere. And it is much livelier and noisier than it used to be. It used to poke along like a kid dragging its feet. Now, it skips along like it had an appointment to keep—like, maybe, it could make an impression on the Pine River laying back in the boondocks. Could be, it seemed, it was "buckin' for promotion." I had remembered it as being petulantly quiet, like a kid that was told to be seen and not heard. Now, it's babbling and verbal, and can be heard to the top of the gully.

White-tail deer "bed down" 'in the flats in winter; the woodchucks chuck all the wood that a woodchuck can chuck; the squirrels keep their memory book up to date about the oak trees; woodpeckers hammer; bluejays yammer; kingfishers honk upstream, and the proud cardinals wouldn't trade their red coats with the Northwest Mounties. During the last year, some beavers built a large dam— like they had read about the Grand Coulee maybe, and the Conservation officers moved them far downstream so they wouldn't flood all the trees in the flats. As the song goes: "Darling, I am Growing Older." No, I couldn't spit across the creek any more. . . . It's amazing how wide the thing's gotten in 40 years.

None of us ever reach the heights we thought we were going to when we left the Old Home Town. We are not the sky-high stalwarts, the sizzling successes, we thought we would become. Maybe it is good for us, if only we remember that at least we aimed high. We never reached the peaks our childhood expected, but at least, once and for all, we saw them. We knew they were there. That is something, and always so good to remember!

— THE END —

# POSTSCRIPT

## SUMMER STOCK

I stood on the hills of where I come from
And looked down upon the land
And there was Summer
Giving it her all
Presenting her Show of Shows.

I watched from the high lonesome
As bright-throated singers
Checked their sheet music
Running the scales before going on.

I, the wind-blown critic
The audience of one
Watched from balconies old and remembered
As Summertime went all out
Putting on her matinee:

A chorus of green corn in perfect rows
On a stage of loam—
Golden wheat fidgeting under a July sun
Waiting for the finale—
White birches whispering lines

*Blow for Batten's Crossing!*

To a blue lake
And the coming, going waves
Unhurried patrons
Ushered by the wind—
Noisy gulls cutting up in the cheaper seats
Dipping, diving
Teasing the sky
Getting their money's worth—
And small-time bit players
The rivers
Padding their parts at sundown.
Everybody wanting Broadway.

Then night dropped the curtain
And the light man went home.

*—Marvin Eugene Girard*